Dream BIGGER

Reclaiming a Life of Joy & Ease

For all your dreams yet to come!

Julie

BY JULIE WISE

iUniverse, Inc.
New York   Bloomington

Dream BIGGER
Reclaiming a Life of Joy and Ease

iUniverse books may be ordered through booksellers or by contacting:

iUniverse
1663 Liberty Drive
Bloomington, IN 47403
www.iuniverse.com
1-800-Authors (1-800-288-4677)

Because of the dynamic nature of the Internet, any Web addresses or links contained in this book may have changed since publication and may no longer be valid.

ISBN: 978-1-4502-5318-5 (sc)
ISBN: 978-1-4502-5320-8 (dj)
ISBN: 978-1-4502-5319-2 (ebk)

Printed in the United States of America

iUniverse rev. date: 9/17/2010

For Matt and Laura

My inspiration for always dreaming bigger

Contents

Introduction

Did you daydream as a child? Do you remember the magic of imagining you could fly like an eagle, or discover new lands like Christopher Columbus, or find a cure for cancer? Perhaps you pictured yourself standing on stage accepting the Nobel Peace Prize, hearing the thunder of applause or savoring the majestic silence from the peak of Mount Everest.

If you stop for a moment and remember what that felt like, chances are you'd describe a sensation of freedom, joy, and ease as well as a strong sense of accomplishment and a deep connection to who you truly are.

This is what it feels like to live our dreams. And, yes, we can experience that today, even if we're all "grown up." That's what this book is all about—learning how to rekindle the magic of dreaming, creating a road map for the journey and moving past the obstacles along the way.

Eight years ago, my dream was to go to Costa Rica. For two years, I'd been setting aside ten percent from every cheque I received for work and putting it into my "dream account" at the bank. That money, saved a few dollars at a time, was enough to cover my flight and accommodation costs for two weeks.

By the end of November that year, I was ready to leave behind the wintry wind and snow-covered ground in Canada to get a new perspective on my life. I was between jobs, involved in a relationship that didn't seem to be going anywhere and had no idea of what to do with my life. A friend invited me to visit her in a small Costa Rican village and, although I didn't know her very well, I decided to take the plunge.

I booked a room at a little hotel on the beach near where my friend lived. Every morning I arose before the sun and took long walks, picking up shells, watching tiny crabs scurry and hide in the sand and enjoying the swooping flight of pelicans over the ocean.

One morning, it was particularly hot, and I really wanted to go swimming. I'd been walking along the edge of the water, feeling the strong pull of the ocean as it ebbed and flowed around my ankles. The water was warm and inviting, but I noticed there was one big wave that I'd need to get past if I wanted to reach the calm water farther out.

I studied the wave from every angle. About ten feet from shore, the seemingly flat water began to rise, gathering momentum and height until it peaked, hovered, and then came crashing down in a single, thunderous, frothing wave, racing toward shore. I watched how other swimmers approached the challenge. Some dove straight into it, emerging with arms flailing in the calmer water on the other side. Others stayed closer to shore, content to paddle in the shallows. Still others tried to go with the flow—waiting for the right timing, jumping up with the wave, and propelling themselves forward with their legs madly kicking as the wave sped past them. However, there were also those who didn't quite make it and tumbled back into shore, only to be marooned on the beach as the water retreated.

As I ventured into the ocean, I was surprised by its powerful tug on my legs, pulling me back toward the shore, and then pushing me deeper out. I had little control over my balance. The water began to lift me off my feet and carry me back and forth. It was a bit scary, so I turned and headed back to the beach.

I didn't see the wave mounting behind me until just before it descended. Instinctively, I stretched out my arms in front of me, tucked my head in between them, and bodysurfed to shore. I flew like a bullet, landing on the beach with such force that my bathing suit was nearly ripped off my body. Lying face down on the sand, with the water rushing over my head, I struggled to get up on my knees and elbows and turn my face upward so I could breathe. The water pummeled me from behind and streamed over me as it ebbed, dragging me back into the ocean. Eyes covered in sand, I clawed my way farther up onto the beach and then rolled onto my back, gasping for air.

I lay there for a few moments wondering what to do. I felt battered and bruised. I wanted to give up, but I also wanted to go swimming. I wasn't going to let a mere wave defeat me. I needed a strategy.

Readjusting my swimsuit, I stood up and strode out into the water. I kept my eyes focused on the wave, allowed my body to float with the ebb and flow of the water, and used my hands to keep myself upright. After watching the wave for a moment, I decided to try and synchronize my movements with the water. As the wave began to build, I leaped forward and began to swim. The water descended, briefly engulfed my head, and then released me like a cork popping off a champagne bottle. I was floating in the stillness behind the wave. Delighted with my boldness, I played there for a while, drifting in the gentle motion of the salty water.

I often think back to that experience when life pulls my feet out from underneath me and brings me to my knees. Events like losing a job, unexpected expenses, health problems, divorce, or the death of a loved one wear us down like a series of tidal waves until we no longer have the strength to stand. It's tempting at that point to give up and let the water gradually bury us in sand so we don't have to face the pressures or stresses anymore. We become shell people—looking the same on the outside, but inside there's emptiness because we've simply disappeared.

Sometimes we find the strength to pull ourselves back up on our knees again, but no farther. Watching from the shore, we resign ourselves to living a half-life. We settle for less because we don't have the energy to try again. We convince ourselves that everything's okay. However, on the inside there is a growing sense of dissatisfaction that never really goes away.

What if there was another way? Instead of giving up on our dreams, or settling for less, what if we stood up, brushed ourselves off, and dreamed bigger? What could happen then?

This book is the result of me dreaming bigger. It is my hope that you will find, within these pages, inspiration, motivation, and practical strategies for reclaiming the life of joy and ease that is your birthright.

I

DREAM

Bloom Where You're Planted

"And the day came when the risk to remain tight in a bud was more painful than the risk it took to blossom."

Anais Nin

Inspiration is found in simple places.

Early in the writing of this book, a friend gave me an amaryllis as a gift. It came in a box with a brightly colored photo of multiple blooms atop tall green stalks. Inside the box, I found a pot, a brown bulb, and a package of dirt. Not very inspiring.

I followed the instructions, planted the bulb in half the soil, and mounded the rest of the dirt up around the top. I watered it and set the pot near my kitchen window. There were a couple of pale white leaf tips showing, but not much else.

Each day when I sat down at the table to write, I'd glance at the plant. At first it didn't seem like anything was happening. Then I noticed that the leaf tips were starting to turn light green and a flat bud seemed to be emerging.

The bud pushed up out of the bulb and grew steadily upward on a thick green stem that seemed to advance by measurable amounts every day. During the night, the stem would lean toward the window, so I had to turn it each morning to keep it growing straight.

Onward and upward, it continued to grow, and all I had to do was water it occasionally. I marveled at its ability to know what it needed to do, and to just do it, without fanfare or struggle. It didn't even need to be noticed. In fact, it would have gone through the same process whether I was in the room or not. Its sole purpose was to grow and blossom, and it did that magnificently.

Finally one day, the stalk stopped growing and the green bud began to split open. Gradually over the course of a week, four dark red flower buds emerged, each one facing a different direction. There was no competing for space or light. They all

3

had exactly enough room to blossom without impeding each other in any way.

I was eager to get to the kitchen in the morning to see the new developments. First one flower opened, wider and wider, and in the following days, the others followed suit. There was no rush or impatience, they took the time needed to fully open and share their beauty in all their glory.

The amaryllis was demonstrating what a life of joy and ease is all about: doing what comes naturally, reaching for what we desire, and celebrating the beauty of our gifts by sharing them with others. I thought about my own life and the struggle and drama we all seem to get caught in as we go through our growth process.

Unlike plants, birds, and animals, we often lose touch with our reason for being here. We become immersed in expectations, demands, stress, and the need to support ourselves. We no longer know how to be ourselves and do what comes naturally.

Our dreams help us reconnect to the essence of who we are. That essence is our true nature. By bringing it into our daily lives, we become more whole, feel more satisfied and fulfilled, and are more enjoyable to be around. Taking our dreams from essence into reality transforms us, and our lives, and changes the world around us in positive ways.

This doesn't mean that our lives will be without challenge and struggle. Life is a learning process and learning occurs through growth and change. However, by staying connected to the essence of who we are, we find more joy and meaning in each day. The transition through the difficult times becomes easier as a result.

Dreaming

"Nothing happens unless first a dream." Carl Sandburg

It all starts with a dream. When the dream connects with enthusiasm, support, and determination, magic happens. However, there may be setbacks along the way, and the path may take us on prolonged detours. I share this next story with you because it illustrates the importance of knowing what you want, being willing to take risks, and having people who believe in you when you lose faith in yourself.

When I was twelve years old, I began to learn French at school. It was my first taste of a foreign language and I loved it. By the end of that year, I had decided on my future—I would become a translator and travel all around the world, meet interesting people, and speak lots of different languages.

To some, this may have seemed like a pretty lofty goal for a young girl from a small rural Ontario town. However, I had supportive parents who told me that, if I worked hard and stayed focused, I could achieve whatever I wanted.

Over the next few years, I pursued my dream with vigor. I took Spanish and Latin, as well as French, in high school and excelled in everything. In grade eleven, my French teacher was from Switzerland and she told me about a world-renowned school of translators and interpreters in Geneva. I was hooked. My new dream was to go to university in Geneva, graduate as a translator in English, French, and Spanish and work at the United Nations.

Determined to succeed, I applied to the University of Geneva as I was finishing my final year of high school. I received a letter from the director saying that most applicants from North America finished an undergraduate degree before applying to the program. He suggested I complete at least two years of a university program in Canada first.

Hopes dashed, I ended up going to Laurentian University in northern Ontario. It had a good translation program, although only in French and English. I promised myself that in two years' time, I would reapply to Geneva.

Life, it seemed, had other plans for me. Within the first year, I met and fell in love with a young man. Halfway through my second year, he proposed and I accepted. We began to plan our marriage and that became my dream. All thoughts of Geneva and working for the United Nations vanished from my head and were replaced by visions of white lace, bridesmaid dresses, and a cozy life for two. He would graduate as a teacher, I would finish my degree, and then I'd look for work as a translator wherever he found a job.

I was blissfully happy. Most of my friends were married; some were starting families; and I now had someone to call my own. I immersed myself in wedding plans between exams and final papers.

I remember a conversation with my mother during this time. My fiancé and I had been home for a visit and he had gone out to run some errands. My mother came and sat beside me with a look that meant we were about to have a "talk."

She hesitated and then spoke.

"Please don't take this the wrong way, dear. You know we like him. He seems like a good person and the two of you seem to have a lot of fun together. But, Dad and I were wondering, does he like to read?"

"What's that got to do with anything, Mom?"

"Well, it's just that you love to read. You've had your nose in a book since you were little. So I guess the question is what he will do with himself while you're reading."

At the time, my parents' concern over something so trivial baffled me. However, I have since realized that they had recognized something I didn't see. There was a serious gap in core values between my fiancé and me, significant enough to lead to potential problems in a long-term relationship.

Fortunately, life intervened once again. About six weeks before our wedding, I discovered that he was having an affair with a friend of mine. Needless to say, I called off the marriage. The rest of the semester passed in a blur. I came home for the summer, lost and unsure of my future. I felt like all my hopes and dreams had been shattered.

My mother, however, remembered my dream of going to Geneva. Unbeknownst to me, she wrote to the university and asked them to send the application forms. When the forms arrived, she handed them to me and simply said, "You're going."

Of course, I resisted. I had a million reasons why it made no sense and why I should just forget about it. After all, I'd just had the bitter experience of having one dream destroyed. Why would I want to set myself up for more disappointment? I'd have to fly to Geneva to write the entrance exams in September and wait there for a month to see if I'd been accepted. There was only a 30 percent acceptance rate at the time. If I wasn't accepted, it would be too late in the year to get into a university program in Canada and what would I do then? Plus there was all the expense. It was too much of a risk as far as I was concerned.

My mother persevered. I applied and was invited to write the entrance exams.

The day came for me to leave. My bags were packed, the airport taxi was waiting in the driveway, and it was time for me to say good-bye. My parents came into my bedroom to see what was taking me so long. I was sitting on the edge of my bed, frozen with fear, unable to get up. Here I was about to take a leap toward a dream I'd had for a decade—a dream I had set aside and forgotten about, and suddenly it was going to become a reality. I began to cry like a little child who's lost in the woods and can't find her way home.

My mother pulled me onto my feet, thrust one suitcase into my hand, and handed the other to my father. She stepped behind me and began to nudge me forward, saying this was no time for nonsense.

"This is your dream and, by golly, you're going to give it all you've got, Julie. We haven't raised you to be a quitter. Now you get in that car, get on that plane, go over there, and show them what you're made of."

And I did. I graduated three years later as a translator, fluent in three languages, with an invitation to write the exams to work at the United Nations. My dream had come true.

Planting the Seed

A dream is a longed-for aspiration; the heart's yearning for "something else," the desire to be or have something that may seem out of reach.

Our dreams and aspirations have the power to inspire, motivate, and excite us. They're fun to think about and even talk about with close friends. However, they are also capable of pushing us into unknown territory, changing our lives, and stretching us beyond what we think is possible. Is it any wonder that most of us either run from our dreams or try to keep them under lock and key?

Dreaming is as natural to us as breathing. When you were a child, did you ever imagine what you might be when you grew up? As an adult, do you ever sit and daydream, staring out the window when you're at work or at home, letting your mind wander, oblivious to the clutter and chaos around you? Those moments give us the chance to pause and reconnect with our true selves and listen to the whisper that reminds us we still have dreams.

We spend most of our waking hours living in consensus reality. That's the world of dishes and laundry, bills and day timers, e-mails and phone calls, schedules and deadlines. The stress and demands can wear us down, leaving us frustrated and angry at the end of the week, snapping at family and resenting our jobs. Weekends are spent trying to get on top of household demands and suddenly it's the workweek all over again. Add to this mix the unexpected loss of a job and much needed income or a family health crisis, and you have a recipe for disaster.

What's missing from this picture? Fun, for one thing. Do you remember what that feels like? That's where dreaming comes in, because in dreaming, we give ourselves permission to be or have whatever we want. There are no limitations or barriers and no rules. However, it's not just about having a good time. It's also about taking steps to move our dreams forward and make them a reality. Spending time developing the dream provides us with the motivation and clarity needed to move past challenges in our day-to-day world and have the life we've always wanted.

We all have dreams. At certain points in our lives, however, our dreams may have become buried by the demands of our lives or tarnished by disappointment. Some dreams change as we grow and evolve, others remain consistent. Sometimes we're so exhausted that our dream is very simple—to have time for a nap.

You may know exactly what your dream is and want to jump ahead to the next section of the book. Please resist this temptation! Each section of this book is like a building block for the next, with valuable tools and insights that interconnect.

For now, we're going to discover together one of your dreams. If you think you don't have any, don't despair. The voice of the dream is still there inside you, even if you haven't heard it for a while.

It's a lot like gardening. First, we need to plant the dream seed in fertile soil. Then, we nurture the seedling so that it grows and thrives. Finally, we reap the benefits of all our work as the dream blossoms and our lives open in new directions.

So, let's get started.

Revealing the Dream

In each section of this book, there are a series of exercises, as well as questions for reflection and action steps. To get the most value out of the book, take your time moving through the exercises. Allow yourself space in which to reflect on where you are and imagine where you want to be.

If you're interested in keeping all your dreamwork work together, I've put together a free downloadable PDF of all the exercises at www.juliewiseconsulting.com/dbx.html

Exercise 1

Please turn off the phone and computer and take steps to ensure that you won't be disturbed. You will need a pen and a pad of paper.

We're going to start with a simple dream, something that you want to bring into your life in the coming weeks. The reason we start slowly is that it's important to build your confidence about dreams coming true for you. There are also skills and tools to learn to help you deal with the challenges along the way. You wouldn't sign up for the Boston Marathon without having taken the time to train, develop your strength and stamina, and experience a few smaller races first, would you?

Sit comfortably with your feet on the floor. Close your eyes and take a few slow deep breaths, becoming aware of your whole body sitting in the chair. Let yourself relax further with each breath. Gently open your eyes and read on.

Imagine that I've just handed you a gift. It's in a small gold box. In your mind's eye, open the box. Inside you'll find a piece of paper that says, "One simple thing I want to bring into my life this month is …"

Say those words out loud and listen for the answer. Write down on the pad of paper the first thing that comes into your head.

Notice if there are judgmental thoughts that surface when you do that. We'll look at that in a moment. For now, remember that in dream world, everything is possible and acceptable.

What do you really want right now? It may be something specific like time for a coffee with a good friend or a long walk in the woods. For some of you, it may be more general like having more time for what you enjoy. Dreams aren't always big and impressive like climbing Mount Everest or ending world hunger. That's why we're starting with what you want *right now*, not six months or a year from now. By learning a simple approach to working with your more immediate desires and needs, you'll gain confidence in applying your skills to bigger long-term dreams. Every dream, no matter how big or small, becomes possible by breaking it down into manageable steps.

Just in case you had trouble coming up with something, let's try another approach.

Remember a time when you felt so excited and happy about something that you could hardly wait to share it with your best friend or a family member. What was it? Write it down. What was so special about it? There is likely a dream buried in that moment. Dig deep, get curious, and see what you can find. It's in there, waiting to be discovered.

Befriending the Gremlins

Now that you've written something down, and had a chance to think about it, there are likely a few unsupportive voices surfacing in your head. You may have had a chorus of comments like:

Don't be ridiculous.
Who do you think you are?
Grow up. Dreams are a waste of time.

Sometimes these voices are more subtle and sneaky:

I don't want to rain on your parade, but remember what happened last time?
I know you're excited, but you really need to be realistic.
Go ahead, give it a try, but don't be surprised when it doesn't work out.
Are you sure that's what you want?

The thoughts might seem logical and practical:

I can't because I don't have the money.
I can't because I don't know how.
I can't because I don't have the time.

Does any of this sound familiar? We all seem to have these inner gremlins, lying in wait for the perfect opportunity to leap up and bring us back to "reality." When we dare to dream, it's like dangling a red cape before a bull. The gremlins line up to launch their attack. The bigger the dream, the more intense their onslaught.

Fortunately, they don't hold as much power as they'd like us to believe.

Exercise 2

Spend a few moments thinking about your dream. Allow it to build until you can picture it coming to life. Where are you?

Who are you with? What are you doing? How are you dressed? Write down some of these details, involving the five senses as much as possible (what you see, taste, smell, touch and hear). How does your body feel right now as you imagine your dream?

Now notice any critical thoughts that are emerging. Write them down as they surface, leaving a couple of lines of space between each thought. Add all the reasons why you can't have this dream. Keep writing until the ideas run out.

Take a look at your list. Read it through carefully, saying each sentence out loud. How does it feel to hear this? Compare this to how you felt when you were imagining your dream.

Critical thoughts are like gremlins skilled in sniper attack. They carefully aim for the weak spots in our defenses and keep firing until we are worn down and disillusioned. At that point, we usually put our dream back on the shelf where it gathers dust indefinitely. We might gaze at it wistfully from time to time, but we rarely do more than that because we're afraid of further disappointment and failure.

This time, however, you're going to use a new tactic. Hidden in every statement on your list is a spark of empowerment. You're going to rewrite each statement to harness its power and use it to your advantage.

For example:

I know you're excited, but you need to be realistic.
It is realistic to want to be happy and to make my dreams come true.

Go ahead, give it a try, but don't be surprised when it doesn't work out.
I will go ahead and be delighted when it DOES work out.

Dreams are a waste of time.
Dreams are essential to a satisfying life.

I can't because I don't know how.
I can because I'll figure it out, or ask someone to help me.

Take each of the critical beliefs on your list and transform them into an empowering statement now.

Playing the Game

Sometimes the gremlins like to play mind games. One of their favorites begins with "what if?" In this next exercise, we're going to explore this game from two different angles.

Exercise 3

Here are a few examples of the kinds of questions gremlins like to slip into our minds:

What if I run out of money?
What if I lose my job?
What if I can't make this idea work?
What if I go back to school and can't handle the workload?

Write down some of the "what if" questions that emerge as you think about your dream. Have you noticed that the "what if" questions always lead to something negative? The impact on us is to raise fears, doubts, and worries, and guess what the purpose of that is? Of course, it keeps us from taking steps toward our dreams.

Now, let's put a twist on the game.

Imagine your dream. Take your "what if" questions and flip them into positive outcomes. For example,

What if I make money doing this?
What if I start a new career as a result of this dream?
What if my idea takes off and is bigger than I'd imagined?
What if I go back to school and love it?

As you ask yourself the question from a positive perspective, notice how your mood and body feel. Questions like this nourish the dream and feed our souls.

Over the next week, play with this idea. Spend time thinking about different aspects of your dream and as the gremlin voices arise, play the "what if" game on them. It's like any other exercise; the more you practice, the easier it will become.

Tracking your Progress

Over the course of a lifetime, we have many dreams that come true. We often forget them or dismiss them as insignificant because we are so focused on the big dreams that didn't work out the way we hoped. We become fixated on attaining one particular goal or achieving a specific measure of success and we lose sight of the accomplishments along the way.

A tool I often use with my clients is a dream journal. It's a small blank journal that has several uses. For now, I'll suggest you use it to write down your moments of success at the end of each day. As you reflect on the day and pay attention to the things that went well, you'll often notice outcomes that surprised you with delight. Even on the most challenging of days, there will usually be at least one bright spot that you can add to your journal.

I'm introducing this concept now because it's an important foundation for the work you'll do in the rest of the book. The road toward your dreams is not always straight and quick. There are bumps, detours, roadblocks, and unexpected exits en route. Sometimes the path is completely buried by an avalanche of rock or snow and you have to make alternative choices and new plans.

The dream journal helps to keep you motivated when things get difficult. As you read back through earlier entries, you'll realize that every day brings something to celebrate. And as you start to focus more on the joy in each day, you'll find the challenges become easier to deal with.

I remember one particular Christmas when my dream journal proved its worth to me. In the weeks leading up to December 25, it felt like my whole world was crumbling around me. My husband and I were separating, although we had agreed to be together for one last Christmas for the sake of our young children. My parents and grandmother had died in the previous few years, so it was my first Christmas without all of them. My grief engulfed me most days. I had been ill for a year and unable to work. My anxiety about how I would pay my bills and give my kids a good Christmas was at its peak. There didn't seem to be any hope of improvement in the near future and I felt completely helpless.

Fortunately, I was working with a life coach at the time, who suggested I start keeping a dream journal. I rolled my eyes at the thought.

"A dream journal? You've got to be kidding. I've got bills to pay and a Christmas to create for my kids. I don't have time for this."

She explained the idea to me and firmly recommended that I give it a try. I was skeptical.

"Look, I already keep a journal. And I write in it every night. It's not helping me change anything, and that's what I really need right now, something to change for the better."

I ended up agreeing to do it, not because I thought it would help, but because I wanted to prove her wrong. After all, what did she know about *my* life?

The first few nights, I opened the journal and stared at the blank pages. What could I possibly find that had been good in the day? My coach had suggested that I start by writing one success, however small it might seem and to write it as a positive statement. I will admit that it took a long time to come up with something at first. However, every night for the first week, I did write down one item. Some nights it was pretty simple.

I survived today. I guess that's success.

In the second week, I started to notice little moments with my children, like when they were playing happily together or when we cuddled up on the couch and read a story together. I was surprised to discover that there were even some good moments with my husband when sharing activities with the children.

We all had fun playing in the snow today.
I made cookies with the kids.

I had a nap while the kids went shopping with their dad.

There were still lots of trying times, tears, and angry discussions. But it didn't get me down like it used to. On rough days, I read through earlier journal entries before I added something new, and each time I was amazed at how many wonderful things had been happening.

It wasn't the best Christmas ever, but there were some good memories in spite of all the challenges we were facing as a family. This is why I recommend to my clients that they keep a dream journal as they prepare to move through any change or transition in their personal or work life.

Dreamwork

In each section of this book, I'll be suggesting dreamwork. It's really another word for homework, but this isn't school or a class you'll be graded on. Instead, this is an activity you can choose to do that will make your overall experience richer and more meaningful as you move through the book.

1. Find a blank lined journal that appeals to you. Choose it because you love the cover, the binding, and the layout of the pages. If you love it, you'll want to write in it every day.
2. At the end of each day, set aside a few minutes to reflect. Think about the day that has just passed. Pick at least one moment that felt good to you. It might be something you did for someone else or someone else did for you. It might be a smile from a stranger or a hug from a good friend. Perhaps you accomplished something, crossed an item off your to-do list, or planned an activity. Start with one and if there are more, keep on writing.
3. Start each morning by expecting something good in the day. Be curious, wonder what it might be, and then pay attention as the day unfolds.

Shifting Perspectives

Sometimes one upsetting event can overshadow all the fulfilling moments that came before it.

I worked with a woman in her fifties who had always dreamed of travelling to China. She had saved her money, booked a tour, and headed off. Just before she was due to return home, she slipped, fell on a crooked step, and broke her ankle. She ended up in hospital in China and came home on crutches. When she came to see me, she was bitter and angry, filled with blame for the tour operator, the surgeons in China, and even God. She was adamant that she would never go on another trip in her life.

"That's what I get for dreaming. Things never work out for me. Why did I think I could actually have what I wanted? Dreams are for fools. I'd have been better off to just stay home. Now, in addition to not being able to walk, I've got all these hospital bills to pay. Why do these things always happen to me? It's just not fair. Other people get to travel and have fun, but not me. There's always something waiting to go wrong."

Over the course of our sessions together, I gently prodded her with questions about different aspects of her trip: people she'd met, places she'd been, and experiences she'd had. I asked her to bring me some photos and together we created a collage of her adventure. As she told me the stories behind the pictures, her face began to light up. She laughed as she shared some of the antics she'd been involved in, and she started to realize how much she had enjoyed the trip itself. She had been depriving herself of that joy and pleasure because of her frustration and anger over the accident.

We weren't able to change the circumstances (her ankle was still broken), but she was able to reconnect to the excitement of travelling. She also mentioned a friend she had made on the flight home, a woman who happened to live in the same town and who loved to travel. This new friend had found wheelchairs and helped her navigate the airports, located her luggage, and even drove her home from the airport. It was a friendship that developed because of her injury.

Pursuing a dream doesn't always have a happy outcome, or even the result that we are hoping for. However, it can offer many unexpected benefits. A lot depends on how you choose to see the experience. Contrary to the example I just mentioned, the woman in the next story was able to look beyond a serious health issue and make the most of her travel dream.

At the age of sixty-five, my mother decided to take a Caribbean cruise with a close friend. In the previous two years, she had lost both her husband and mother, and the trip was her way of bringing some joy back into her life. She had always wanted to travel, and she hoped this would be the first of many opportunities to see the world.

Two weeks before they were due to leave, she collapsed in the front hallway of her house while sweeping the floor. A friend found her and called the ambulance. After taking x-rays and running some tests, her doctor told her that she appeared to have a shadow on one of her lungs. He said it was probably a touch of pneumonia, prescribed antibiotics and painkillers, and insisted that she carry on with her travel plans. He asked her to come see him after the trip and said he would give her the complete test results at that time.

It was, in fact, terminal lung cancer. The doctor was fully aware of this and wanted to ensure that my mother had a chance to enjoy the trip before she had to deal with reality of dying. To this day, I bless him for his wisdom.

My mother went on the cruise. She was in pain every time she took a breath because the tumor had grown beyond her lung and had broken some ribs. However, with the aid of painkillers, her supportive friend, and her own determination, she had a wonderful time. She came back with photos, gifts, and many stories of people she had met.

During her follow-up visit with the doctor, she learned the truth and was told she had about one year to live. However, in spite of growing pain, exhaustion, and waning physical strength, she packed more memories into that year than most people experience in a lifetime.

What's the Point?

It's often easier to come up with reasons not to pursue our dreams than it is to find good reasons to give it a try. Some of the more common obstacles that get in our way involve fear or lack of something.

You might be afraid that things won't work out and you'll be disappointed—again. Or you might be afraid that things *will* work out and it will change the relationships or circumstances in your life. Some people mention a lack of money, time, or skills as being the reasons they can't have their dreams. For others, it's a lack of self-worth. They believe that they don't deserve to have dreams come true, perhaps because they feel they haven't worked hard enough yet or because it's not their "turn."

Whatever the reasons, they are nothing more than a smoke screen, cleverly raised by our inner gremlins to keep us in check and maintain the status quo. Their reasoning is that, even if we're unhappy with our current situation, it's much better to play it safe. Why risk trying something new and unknown? Their tactics often work, causing us to put off our plans, telling ourselves and others that we'll do it when:

- We have more time.
- We have more money.
- Our children are older.
- We retire.
- We've paid off the mortgage.
- We get a new job.
- We get a raise.

The list goes on and on.

The question we need to ask ourselves is this: "What risk am I taking by putting my dreams on hold?"

*****

A friend of my family had always wanted to be an archeologist. However, when she was young, there was no money for a university education. Instead she married and focused on being a good wife and mother and tried to feed her dream by reading library books about ancient civilizations. After her children were grown and her husband died, she discovered a program in which seniors could study inexpensively at universities around the world. She began to make plans to go on an archeological dig in Greece, only to be diagnosed with a terminal illness. She died before she could go.

The impact of waiting can be subtle. It wears away at us, day by day, gradually eroding our connection to the essence of who we are the way a waterfall eats away at the underlying rock. At first, we might notice how we erupt into frustration and anger as our emotions become more raw and exposed. Over time, we begin to feel numb. We become a shadow figure, going through the motions of our lives, playing a role, but no longer actively participating in the world around us. It's as if we've disappeared, although our bodies are still physically present. The look in our eyes is vague and listless, and nothing excites us anymore. These are all signs that we've lost touch with the dream.

When we give up on our dreams, we give up on ourselves. This doesn't just affect our own lives; it also affects the lives of those around us.

I recently worked with a woman who had been through a particularly difficult year. Her husband had been sidelined with a serious hip injury that had required surgery and a lengthy recovery period, and it still wasn't healing. For a year, she had been driving him back and forth to work out of town, taking their young children to school and various activities in between working part-time and keeping the household running. They had just found out that he would require further surgery and would likely be unable to walk or drive for at least another six months. She was angry, bitter, and frustrated, given to sudden explosive outbursts, and ready to break down. She recognized that the ongoing stress was affecting her relationships as well as her own health, and something needed to change. However, she couldn't see any options, nor could she see any hope in the future.

As we talked, I realized that her conversation was like a never-ending tape that circled around and around with the same message. She sat hunched in the chair with her arms and legs crossed, staring at the floor. The situation was unfair, the doctors were incompetent, she couldn't take it anymore, but she didn't have any choices. I asked her to close her eyes and take some slow deep breaths. Then I asked, "What do you want more than anything right now?"

Without hesitation, she replied, "Time out. Where I don't have to think or do anything for anyone." I told her that I'd just wiped her slate clean and she could have that time. Then I asked, "Where do you see yourself having this time?"

She quickly responded, "At a beach."

We explored the details of the setting and how it felt to be there. As we talked, I periodically checked in to see how she was feeling. She was gradually relaxing, breathing more deeply, and stretching out her arms and legs.

I explained that she could have this dream in her life right now. She looked at me in disbelief. After all, it was December and there was snow on the ground outside the office. We explored how it could happen. She decided that she could give herself two hours off two days a week to lie on her bed, put on a headset, and listen to a CD of nature sounds, letting her body sink into the mattress as she imagined herself resting on a warm beach.

In order to make it possible, she said she would cross the time off in her day planner and let her family know that she was not to be disturbed during that time, "unless the house is on fire." She stated her commitment out loud and repeated the details to me before she left. When we checked in a few days later, she said she was feeling much calmer.

"I realize I've been trying to change the circumstances and I can't," she said. "It's been like hitting my head against a wall. Now I'll focus my energy on taking care of myself. That will make it easier to handle whatever lies ahead."

Time for Reflection

Do you recognize the signs of a forgotten or postponed dream in yourself or others? Take heart, because there are easy steps that will reconnect you with your soul's desires.

It's time for some quiet reflection. Take a pen and pad of paper and jot down the ideas that come to you as you ask yourself the following questions. There is no right or wrong answer; trust that the ideas that come to you are what you are ready to work with.

Think of one dream that you've never allowed yourself to pursue. Write it down.

1. How would your life change if that dream came true?
2. What is getting in your way?
3. What would you need to let go of in order to move toward that dream?

Now think of a time when one of your dreams became a reality. Write it down.

1. What was your first reaction (thoughts, emotions, sensations in your body)?
2. What happened next?
3. How was your life affected?

Check-in

As we move through this book, we will stop periodically to check in. The check-in for this section is about self-awareness. Moving toward our dreams can bring up old issues of fear and disappointment, mistaken beliefs, and worried thoughts. Just when we think we've dealt with the gremlins, another one can surface. So it's important to take stock occasionally to see how you're feeling and what you might need to do to support yourself in moving forward.

Pause for a moment, put the book down, and check to see how your body and mind are doing right now. If you just finished the reflection questions, did they trigger any reaction (positive or negative)? Are you feeling calm and inspired, or anxious and afraid?

Make a note of how you are feeling. If there are challenges surfacing, what do you need in order to deal with them? Perhaps you need to take some time out and do something else for a while. Maybe you need to work on the gremlins exercises again. Or you might need to go back to the first exercise where you identified your dream, so that you can feel inspired again.

Find a way to create the support you need right now, before you go any farther in the book. Remember that the path to our dreams is not straight and narrow. It's always shifting and evolving, just as we are. It takes self-awareness, self-mastery, a good support system, and a solid action plan to get us to where we dream of being.

Moving into Action

Dreams are just dreams until we take action to make them real. However, it's important to spend time in the dreaming phase so that we can identify the dream and then come up with appropriate steps to bring it to life. In the first exercise, you identified a dream. Then you worked at eliminating the inner obstacles to moving that dream forward. In the third exercise, you gave yourself permission to make it happen. Dreamwork, the reflective questions, and the check-in provided nourishment and support to your dream. All of these steps moved you forward from dreaming to consensus reality.

Now let's develop an action plan for the dream you identified in Exercise 1.

1. What do you want to bring into your life this month? Check back to see what you wrote down in Exercise 1.
Be specific about what you want. Add in as many details as you can. For example, you may want time for coffee with a friend. Describe who the friend is, where you'd like to meet, the time of day, and for how many hours. Write down how soon you want this to happen. Picture what you will be wearing. Imagine what you'll talk about, hear the laughter, feel the warmth of the coffee cup in your hands, smell the aroma in the air. Write a note about what it feels like to be there.

2. What are the challenges getting in your way? Make a list based on what you wrote for Exercise 2.
Using the same example, you might be having difficulty finding the time because of work and family commitments. Perhaps your friend lives out of town or works nights and weekends. You may believe that it isn't worth making the effort because you've tried before and it has never worked out. You might be a single parent with young children, and you don't feel comfortable leaving your children with a sitter while you go out.

Whatever your challenges are, write them down.

3. What are your fears? Write down the first group of "what if" questions from Exercise 3.

Fears can trick us into believing that nothing is possible. By writing them down, we get them out of our heads and out on paper where we can deal with them. As long as they remain in our minds, they swirl round and round, building in size and strength until we feel paralyzed. Write them down so you can see for yourself what you're dealing with.

Using the example above, your fears might be expressed in the following ways:

"What if I can't find a good sitter?"
"What if something happens to my kids while I'm out?"
"What if my friend and I can't find a time that works for both of us?"
"What if I make all these arrangements and then she has to cancel?"

4. What kind of support do you need to deal with your challenges and fears? Make a list of your needs.

This is where you need to set aside your emotions and use your logical mind. Take a look at the list of challenges and fears. Imagine for a moment that you are solving a puzzle for a complete stranger. When you read through the list, what can you see that is needed?

In the above case, for example, this person needs:

- To get in touch with her friend and find out when she might have some available time
- To come up with a couple of possible dates to meet
- To find a sitter for her children so she can enjoy the time with her friend
- To find someone to keep her motivated

5. Where can you find the resources to meet your needs? Be creative. Think about family, friends, community services, and your own skills and abilities.

Look at your list of needs and come up with one way of meeting each need. In our example, she may be able to find another friend or family member to stay with her children for an hour or two while she goes for coffee. In preparation, she could ask the sitter to spend time with the children now so that they are comfortable by the time the coffee date arrives. She could share her dream with a close friend or family member and ask them to help her stay motivated or to offer new ideas if the arrangements get challenging. She can also let her friend know how important it is to get together, so that the friend is making a serious effort to make it happen too.

6. What steps are in your action plan? When you look at your list of possible resources, you will notice that there are actions embedded in the list. Pull out the actions and create your action plan.

Here is an action plan for our example:

- Send an email to her friend to let her know how much she wants to get together. Ask for a couple of dates/ times that might work for her.
- Ask friends, family, and neighbors for the name of a good sitter.
- Meet with sitters, do an interview, ask for references.
- Pick a sitter and have her spend time with the children while she's still at home.
- Get the sitter to stay with the children while she goes out for a short time.
- Let her best friend know that she's doing all this and ask her to check in periodically to keep her motivated.
- Ask for help if she's running into challenges.

7. What is one action you can take today toward your dream?

Before you start taking action, it's important to give yourself a time line. When do you want to have accomplished your goal? Now take the steps in your action plan and spread them out between today and the end date.

Take the first step of your action plan today.

Congratulations! You're on your way toward making a dream come true.

Keeping the Momentum Going

Each time you take a step from your action plan, mention it in your dream journal. Writing it down reinforces the strength of the action and builds your momentum. As with any journey toward a dream, whether big or little, complex or simple, you may trip and stumble from time to time. That's a normal part of the process, and it happens to all of us. The people who reach their dreams are those who didn't let those tumbles stop them.

In the next section, you'll learn in more detail how to stay motivated and keep the momentum going. For now, here are three points to remember:

1. **Keep your focus on your dream.**
2. **Ask for help and support when you need it.**
3. **Believe, believe, believe.**

When things get challenging, go back to your description of your dream and what it would feel like to have it happen. Close your eyes and spend some time experiencing those wonderful feelings. It's a bit like recharging your inner batteries so you can take more steps. This is an easy way to stay focused.

Sometimes we can't make things happen by ourselves. We need the support, knowledge, or expertise of other people. So don't hesitate to ask for help. Keep in mind that no one can make the dream come true for us. That part is up to us. However, as long as we're willing to make the effort, others are usually happy to provide some support. Be specific about what you need and what the time commitment is in order to make it easier on your support team.

It all comes down to believing—in ourselves, in our dreams, and in the possibility of having dreams come true. We can dream all we want, take lots of action, but if we honestly believe it's not going to happen, then it won't. We'll explore this in more detail in the next part of the book because it is a common issue. For now, start to notice any thoughts or beliefs that surface in your mind as you take steps toward your dream and jot them down.

To inspire you further, here are two stories about people whose dreams took on a life of their own and grew beyond their expectations, making a difference in the world around them.

Onward and upward!

DREAMMAKERS

Inspiring stories of people
whose dreams make a
difference in the lives of
others

Derek Lucas,
REC for Kids

Amy Peterson,
Grandmothers Beyond Borders

Derek Lucas: Making Dreams Real

Dreams don't have to be complicated. Sometimes they start from a simple desire to make a difference in the local community. When the idea is communicated to others, it gains support and grows into a wellspring of community involvement that catches even the dreamer by surprise.

When Derek Lucas retired in 2006 after fifty years in the telecommunications industry, he had an idea percolating in the back of his mind. He wanted to give away sports equipment to children in need so that everyone could have a healthy, active, and fun childhood regardless of income. The concept was modeled after a program in Edmonton, Alberta, where some of his former work colleagues volunteered.

"Sports Central had been going for about seventeen years," he explained. "It began as a group of friends collecting hockey equipment from their neighbors and giving it away to children from the trunks of their cars. I wondered why there was only one organization like it in Canada and I was determined to make it happen here."

Derek made a presentation to his Rotary Club in southern British Columbia, and after a feasibility study and a trip to Edmonton to visit Sports Central, Rotary's REC for Kids began.

REC stands for Recycle Equipment and Cycles, and that's what the program does. Good quality used sports equipment is donated and given away for free. Derek points out that many area families cannot pay the prices even at used equipment stores, so REC fills the gap. REC for Kids has the first choice of bikes that are picked up around the city by the police, so they are used in the bike repair program. Helmets are purchased through a donation from area firefighters. Hockey sticks and mouth guards are also bought new and given away.

Children and youth are referred to the program by social service organizations, the police, and area school boards. The REC executive director makes appointments with the families to come in to pick up what their children need from available stock.

The program has blossomed since its inception, with broadening community support that now includes members of three Rotary Clubs in the area as well as municipal, community, and private sponsors. A local social services program decided to partner with a bike shop and REC to set up a training course for at-risk youth. Upon high school graduation, these teens attend a six-week program at REC for Kids and receive a bike repair certificate. They build a bike from parts for themselves and repair other bikes for REC to give away.

The Youth Intervention branch of the Royal Canadian Mounted Police is another strong supporter of the program. Derek gave an example.

"There was a youth who was caught stealing bikes. But the officer recognized that he also had a gift for repairing bikes. So he recommended that (as an alternative justice plan) the boy build a bike for the kid he'd stolen from and build one for himself."

This is when life offered an interesting twist to the story. On the first day of the course, the boy whose bike had been stolen also showed up. Apparently he'd been referred to the program through social services because he was an at-risk youth. Only the course leaders were aware of the situation and handled it smoothly.

The whole approach of REC for Kids is based on respect and the idea of giving a hand up, not a handout. Families are given individual appointments so that their time is private and confidential. The best equipment in the size of the child is brought out to them for fitting. If the executive director discovers that a child is interested in street hockey, she'll give out an old hockey stick and tennis ball as well. When children go downstairs to look at the bikes, there's one waiting in their size with their name already on it. They also receive a helmet and a lock, as well as a clear explanation about the responsibility of looking after their equipment.

The philosophy behind the program isn't limited to what happens within the walls of the building. One day, a REC volunteer noticed a couple of teenagers playing basketball on a court behind the building with an old ball that had almost no air in it. He went back into REC for Kids, found a well-inflated ball and gave it to the two young men. They were brothers who had just arrived in Canada from the Philippines, didn't know anyone yet, but loved to play basketball. They were amazed that someone would simply give them a good ball.

For Derek, this is a good example of the importance of involving children in sports. He feels it gives them a better chance of staying "on the straight and narrow." In a province where 1 in 5 children are raised below the poverty line, sports participation is not a financial option for many families. As a result, REC for Kids has handed out over 350 pieces of equipment to more than 50 children in its first year of operation.

"We'd like to see it grow faster," he says. "We'd like to see the program become redundant, so we're not needed. But we need to build the dream, one step at a time."

This process does take time, energy, and support. One of the biggest obstacles at the start was overcoming funding challenges. Most foundations want to give money to something tangible, not for operations.

"Everything is donated, and we give everything away," he explains, "so all of our costs are for operations. It would have been easier to raise money if we were actually buying all the equipment."

The core group was not deterred, though, and persevered with the encouragement and expertise of the Sports Central program in Edmonton. The executive director there shared his experience with the team and offered to support them in any way he could. He even offered to send along some of their surplus equipment if needed for their opening.

Such support is key to making a dream real, according to Derek. It's also important to do your homework before you start as with any business.

"Write a business plan, and use it as your Bible," he says. "Find the best people there are around you, make sure they share your dream, and get them involved. Get the support of two or three outside groups as well. And remember that failure is not an option."

He admits that his involvement in REC for Kids has changed his life and opened his eyes to real community needs. He now sees troubled youth and people living on the street as people he wants to reach. He suggests that it's time to practice locally what we preach internationally and work toward meeting the day-to-day needs of families. He also feels the focus needs to be on the children.

"The Olympics in Vancouver helped," he says. "People saw kids who chose sports and reached the pinnacle. They saw that not all kids do drugs, steal cars, or do graffiti. You can change children."

He still remembers the expression on the face of the little girl to whom he gave the first bike on the opening day of REC for Kids. The look of excitement in her eyes is what motivates him to move forward with this program. His advice to others is simple.

"Don't dream on a small scale. Dream big!"

For more information: www.recforkids.com

Amy Peterson: Heart Wisdom

Inspiration comes from unexpected sources: a fragment of a conversation overheard in a store, the lyrics to a song, a news item on the television all hold the potential to touch your heart and mind and move you to action.

A few years ago, Amy Peterson was driving down the road in Milwaukee, Wisconsin, listening to the radio. She heard the story of a woman in Uganda who had lost all fourteen of her children to AIDS and was raising her ten grandchildren on her own in poverty.

"I was blown away," she says. "I started thinking about my own grandmother and my mother, and how much we have here. It made me pause. And then my mind started thinking about how grandmothers can support each other."

When she got home, she called a friend. One thing led to another and the concept of Grandmothers Beyond Borders was formed. The aim of the organization is to improve the lives of grandmothers and grandchildren struggling to survive because of the impact of AIDS. In Uganda, it is estimated that grandmothers care for about 45 percent of children whose parents have died of AIDS.

Amy is quick to admit that she knew nothing about international work or even Africa at the start.

"We realized that we needed to educate ourselves, so my daughter and I went to Uganda. We interviewed thirty-four grandmothers and one grandfather who were raising their grandchildren. We came back to the U.S. to share their stories, although we had no idea at the time that we would eventually become a nonprofit organization."

Her twenty-three-year-old daughter took photos to document the journey. Amy recalls feeling out of her element and overwhelmed by shock. Her initial vision was to simply meet with the grandmothers and gather their stories.

"I wanted them to know they're not alone, that I heard their story and was touched by it. I didn't know what we could do about it, but I thought that by learning more about the scope of the problem, maybe something would emerge."

The Ugandan grandparents could not believe that these two women had travelled 9,000 miles just to hear their story.

"I remember sitting with them in their huts. Just thinking about it now moves me to tears," she says. "We had to have a translator, but in a way, we spoke the same language—the language of the heart."

When they returned to the United States, Amy hoped to connect the Ugandan grandmothers with local grandparents raising their grandchildren. That didn't work out. Instead, other grandparents stepped up after hearing the stories. Doors opened, volunteers came forward, and fund-raising began.

A year later, Amy went back to Uganda. In the interim, the grandmothers there had formed an elders association, picked leaders, and created a regular meeting structure. They had located all the grandparents in the outskirts and formed collectives with the support of Caritas, an international humanitarian aid organization.

Fund-raising for the four Ugandan villages takes place in the United States, with each village receiving equal amounts of funding, and the village associations decide how the money will be spent. They make regular reports, and volunteers from Grandmothers Beyond Borders visit once a year.

During the most recent visit, volunteers realized that elders are spending long days walking out to visit the grandmothers who cannot make it to monthly meetings because of age or illness. Two bicycles were donated to each village in order to keep everyone connected more easily.

Amy explains that the goal is for the villages to become independent. Funding to date has been for small community-based needs such as pig and poultry projects, bedding, and food baskets. One village is currently forming a women's collective so they can apply for local government funding for bigger projects.

According to Amy, the biggest challenge so far is understanding the cultural implications of their visits.

"Given the history of colonization and what's been taken out of Africa by Western governments, I don't think we realized the risk of raising expectations just by being there," she says. "We have to think carefully about what we say and how we say it, and to look at what we really can do, and not make promises we can't keep."

Everyone who works with Grandmothers Beyond Borders is a volunteer, and many have full-time jobs elsewhere. Amy, who is the executive director, has a full-time job at the Archdiocese of Milwaukee. Sometimes she wishes she could do more, but has come to recognize that it's important to look at all that has been accomplished.

"I come back to the heart of the project," she explains, "which is about being in solidarity with these women. Whatever we're able to do, it's okay. It helps to keep things in perspective."

She stresses the importance of having support, suggesting that others need to be invited to carry and hold the dream with you. These are people who are willing to be there for you when things are going well and when they're not. She points out there is a reciprocal benefit involved.

"There are so many good people who want to contribute. You don't have to do it alone. And when you invite others to share in your dream, you're also inviting them to touch their own."

She suggests that another key to success is staying focused on the reason you became involved in the first place. Your heart knows the answer to this.

"For me, it's the grandmothers and women around the world who suffer," she says. "My dream is to make the world a better place. What happens to others affect us. My call is to work with women who are oppressed and hurting. They are my sisters, mothers, and grandmothers. And now that I have a grandchild of my own, this experience gives a whole new meaning to being a grandmother."

For more information: www.grandmothersbeyond.org

II

DREAM BIG

Believe It or Not

When I was a child, I remember reading the fable about Chicken Little. In the story, a chicken is eating lunch one day, when an acorn falls on her head from the tree above her. She believes the sky is falling and runs around spreading the word about impending disaster.

Chicken Little jumped to a conclusion and assumed the worst. How many of us do that on a regular basis? Our inability to believe in ourselves and our dreams often stops us from trying to create a better life for ourselves. When we hit an obstacle, we give up because "it was crazy to think I could do it." If someone tells us that we're foolish or reaching beyond our means, we believe the words and stop trying. Even when something goes well, we downplay our success and focus on the one small detail that went wrong.

My mother used to worry continuously about what might happen. I teased her about having to find something to worry about even when things were going well. She told me she was afraid to be happy "because something always goes wrong." Her faith in goodness had been shattered by experiences that had occurred when she was young. As a result, like Chicken Little, she was always running around trying to shield herself and her family from what "could" happen.

She no longer believed in possibilities for herself. Instead, she channeled all her energy into making my dreams come true, perhaps to compensate for what hadn't happened in her own life. In spite of this support, I managed to inherit some of her pessimism toward life, believing that there was a limit on how much joy I could have. Every time something went wrong, it reinforced this belief. I reached a point where I began to believe that she might have been right about life.

During a particularly dark period, my attitude became "I expect the worst, and that way I won't be disappointed." I thought that was the only option under the circumstances. You

47

know what? It didn't help. I felt more and more disappointed at the way my life was going, and the worst part was that I couldn't find anyone to blame.

If Chicken Little had taken the time to look up, or to consult with someone wiser than she was, she could have saved herself and her friends a lot of unnecessary stress and anguish. It took me a long time to reach this awareness. Like Chicken Little, I was convinced that I knew all there was to know about life and the way it works, and I didn't need any help, thank you very much! As I result, I floundered and struggled for years, feeling bitter and frustrated that I seemed destined for such despair.

I was too proud to ask for help. I'd always been independent and stubborn, so it took me a very long time and much disaster, before I was finally ready to raise the white flag and say, "I surrender." There had been support around me all that time, but I was unwilling to see it or make use of it.

Sources of information, support, and wisdom surround us at all times. The hardest part may be admitting, to ourselves and to others, that we don't know it all. Asking and reaching out for help may seem like a sign of weakness to some, yet it's an act of strength. We're acknowledging that we're part of a larger community. We have gifts to offer to others, just as they may have what we're seeking in that moment.

There is strength in numbers, so in reaching out you'll find that your burden gets lighter. Friends, family, colleagues, acquaintances are usually happy to help out once you know what you want. You do need to be ready to move forward though. People are not going to help you stay stuck in a rut of misery.

As I got back on my feet, and things started to improve, I had to remind myself of Chicken Little. Instead of expecting the worst or assuming that everything would inevitably fall apart again, I decided to expect the best. It wasn't easy at first, because it meant breaking the old thought patterns that came so easily to me. I focused on noticing and appreciating all the wonderful moments that occurred every day. I made a point of thanking those who were supporting me and offering some of my time and gifts to them in return. In this way, we created a circle of goodness that kept flowing among and around us.

I was surprised by how much easier my life began to feel, and I noticed that, for the first time in years, I was starting to dream again. Possibilities were emerging that I'd long since given up on. It was because I was allowing myself to give to, and receive from, a supportive community.

I like to think of us as part of a global tapestry. Each thread is unique in color, texture, age, and strength. They are woven together in a certain order to create a work of art that is constantly evolving, shifting, changing. Yet no single thread is the tapestry. Together, with our combined beauty, we are a masterpiece.

What aspect of beauty do you have to bring to the tapestry of life? Remember, your gifts are unique to you. No one else can voice your story, manifest your dream, or share your wisdom with the world.

Inside you, there is a dream that wants to be heard. Perhaps you've not given it a chance because you've been told to be practical and realistic. Maybe you tried once, but ran into some difficulties and gave up, telling yourself that at least you gave it a shot. What is standing in the way of your dream today?

What are you going to do about it?

Dreaming Big

"Build a dream and the dream will build you." Robert H. Schuller

Sometimes you have to hit bottom before you're willing to take a risk and try something new.

I remember the night I considered suicide. I'd been sick with chronic fatigue syndrome for four years by then. I was running out of money, unable to work because of physical and mental pain and exhaustion, and had just been turned down for disability insurance. My marriage had ended three years prior, and my children were living primarily with their father. I was depressed, I was isolated from friends and family because the sound of conversation jarred my entire nervous system, and I was barely able to take care of my basic needs.

Eyes closed, I sat in the dark in the living room that night holding my throbbing head in my hands. All of my joints ached, my legs felt as heavy as concrete blocks, and my mind was weary from trying to figure out what to make for supper. I'd had day after day of pain and exhaustion, and there didn't seem to be any hope of improvement—ever.

I felt like crying but didn't have the energy to make tears. I concentrated on breathing, inhaling and exhaling, marveling that my body was able to keep air moving through my lungs even when I could no longer move without great effort.

I noticed wisps of words threading slowly through my mind. *Why … bother? What's … the … point? It's never … going … to get … any … better.* It was like hearing the soundtrack to a movie at half-speed, a bit garbled and sluggish, barely comprehensible.

Listening, I began to wonder if I had any choices. This wasn't living, it was merely surviving, and that wasn't what I wanted. It didn't look like things were going to get any better. So maybe I should just end the suffering. As my mind wrapped around this thought, another emerged … how do you do that?

I pushed my brain to sort this out. Then I realized that no matter what method I might come up with, I didn't have the physical or mental energy to carry it out. There I was, not wanting to live, but not able to die. I sighed in despair.

I gradually realized that I had no choice but to live. And if that were the case, then I'd have to eat. I edged forward on the couch and gingerly pushed myself onto my feet. I shuffled out to the kitchen to make supper. It took a couple of hours, because I needed to lie down and rest in between tasks, but I did it. Although I didn't know it at the time, that was the first step toward creating a new dream for myself.

A couple of years passed, and I began to recover with the support of a naturopath. As I grew stronger, I looked for work that would be flexible enough to allow me the option of resting on days when my symptoms resurfaced. At first, I put my artistic talents to use, creating designs on walls in homes and businesses. I enjoyed the flexible hours, the creativity, and the positive feedback from my clients, but it wasn't enough income to fully support me. I knew I needed something with more regular hours.

An ad appeared in the local newspaper for a part-time reporter. I had good writing skills, so I decided to apply although I was nervous. Was I well enough to handle a steady part-time job?

I spent the first three months doing interviews, writing articles, and taking photos. It felt good to be out in the community, reconnecting with people again. I was surprised at how healthy I seemed to be. Then the editor called me into her office and told me she was planning on leaving. Was I interested in taking over her position?

I thought about it for a few days. This was a dream I'd always had—to support myself as a writer—and yet I was afraid that my health wasn't strong enough to handle the demands of full-time hours. I decided to take the chance.

I worked there for two years and built the newspaper into a vibrant, active part of the community. I thrived on meeting people, gathering stories, and sharing them with readers. For me it was an opportunity to create awareness, build relationships among residents, and develop a stronger sense of community connectedness. However, the long hours began to take their toll, and I knew it was time to move on to something else.

I gave my notice at the newspaper without knowing what I would do next. I wanted to continue writing, working with the community, have flexible hours, and make more money. That wasn't much of a job description though, and I only had enough money saved to support myself for about a month.

One of my last interviews was with a high-profile community figure who was heading up a new project. When I mentioned I was leaving the newspaper, he asked what I was planning on doing next.

"I have no idea, but if you hear of something, let me know."

On the last day of work, just before I was due to leave, the phone rang. It was the man I'd interviewed two days earlier.

"Would you be interested in some consulting work?" he asked. "We've already hired a consultant for this project, but we need someone like you who's well connected in the community. It would only be for a few months, but if you're interested, let me know."

And so, I became a consultant. Over the next few years, I worked on numerous projects, writing, researching, organizing, planning and coordinating small and large groups, facilitating meetings and workshops, using all my skills and experiences in ways I'd never dreamed possible. One opportunity led to another, and eventually I found myself working on a project in Argentina for a few months. I'd come a long way from that night on the couch when I thought I had nothing left to live for.

As I look back, I can see that our dreams have more power than we realize. Even when we're not aware of it, they are nudging us in new directions. As we grow and change, our dreams grow with us, gradually gaining momentum until they take us places we hadn't envisioned for ourselves.

It pays to dream and dream big.

Seeing the Signs

We're not always conscious of our dreams at first. In the story I just related, I didn't start out with the dream of being a consultant in Argentina! During my illness, that idea would have seemed pretty farfetched. All I wanted to do was find enough energy to make supper. Yet the spark of a dream existed deep inside me, in spite of the darkness of my circumstances. That tiny flame was enough to get me up off the couch and into the kitchen that night and to keep me moving over the following years. Even when I was unsure of my abilities, the ember of a dream prompted me to say yes to opportunities and to take a chance.

The dream itself may have been undefined, yet it inspired me to take steps. As long as those steps moved me forward, I was reaching for something better, a new beginning, a fresh start.

I point this out because we don't always know what we want. I've had clients comment that it's often easier to figure out what they *don't* want than what they do want. It's important to recognize that knowing what you don't want is a good step toward clarifying what you want. It's a way of narrowing down the possibilities, and that's progress!

Even when we're not clear about our dream or the direction in which we want to head, it's essential to remember that the answers we're seeking do exist already, deep inside us. If we're patient with our own growth process, and we're willing to listen to the hints that come to us through our thoughts, we will find our way toward the life we want.

Our thoughts and our reactions to them are powerful indicators of dreams-in-waiting. Have you noticed how excited you feel about certain ideas and yet you're completely bored by others? Do you ever have a seemingly random thought about going somewhere or calling someone? When that happens, do you follow through or ignore the thought? Are there sections of a newspaper that you always read or television channels that you prefer?

We are constantly surrounded by information about ourselves, our preferences, and our passions, but we're often so caught up in our day-to-day world that we fail to notice the signs. However, we can learn to pay attention, to harness the power of our thoughts, and to channel this energy toward changing our lives.

You've already learned the basic steps in dreaming and bringing the dream to life. In this section of the book, we're going to focus on discovering our hidden dreams, having the courage to bring them forward, and staying motivated in the face of challenges.

Reawakening your Potential

Once upon a time, in a world far away, there was a young child. This child had a wonderful gift—a vivid imagination. The child played with the gift every day and had a lot of fun. Everything was possible. Everything was within reach.

This child is you.

Exercise 1

We're going to travel back in time for a moment and see what we can discover. It's important to set aside some focused time for these exercises. Please turn off the phone and computer and take steps to ensure that you won't be disturbed. You will need a pen and a pad of paper.

Sit comfortably with your feet on the floor. Close your eyes and take a few slow deep breaths, becoming aware of your whole body sitting in the chair. Let yourself relax further with each breath. Open your eyes and read on.

Picture yourself as a young child. Write down the first thoughts that come to mind in response to these questions:

- What kinds of things did you enjoy doing?
- Who were your best friends, and why?
- What was your favorite activity?
- What did you want to be when you grew up?

Now let's move forward to when you were ten to twelve years old. Write down your first thoughts in response to the same questions.

Do the same thing for your teenage years.

Take a look at your notes. Make a note of any pattern or theme emerging. See if there is a common thread that runs through all of those age groups.

Try to set aside any critical thoughts or "gremlins" that may be surfacing because there is one more question to answer.

Without hesitation, write down the first thing that comes to mind when I ask:

"What have you always wanted to be?"

Go ahead, write it down! It can be our secret for now, okay?

******

When I was a little girl, I wanted to be a writer. I wrote my own stories and poems, taped or stapled the pages into "books," added illustrations and cover pages, and proudly put my name on the front. As I grew older, I excelled in English class, especially at writing essays. I was an avid reader as well. Yet, I didn't become a writer. I grew up believing that writing wasn't practical and I needed to find something more realistic to do with my life.

Nonetheless, the dream persisted. I kept setting it aside, tried to ignore it, but it always resurfaced. In my spare time, I wrote a newspaper column for a few years, lots of poetry and stories (most of which I didn't even try to publish), and even the draft of two books. However, it wasn't until much later, after some life-changing experiences, that I finally accepted the dream as an essential part of who I am and chose to invest my time and energy in making it a reality.

It was hard for me to admit to it, almost like admitting that I had an addiction or a weakness of some sort. I think I expected people to laugh or poke fun at me, yet those closest to me were simply surprised that it had taken me so long to figure it out. To them, it had been obvious all along.

When I look back, I can see how the thread wove through my entire life, sometimes fading and almost disappearing, but always there. The dream didn't give up on me, even though I often gave up on it. Dreams are like that.

Nourishing the Dream

When you plant a seed in the ground, you don't just walk away and forget about it, do you? It will probably survive, given some rain, warmth, and sunshine, but it won't necessarily flourish. The same is true of our dreams. Once we identify them, if we really want them to thrive, then we need to take steps to feed and nurture them.

Of course, dreams don't grow on rain, warmth, and sunshine. But they do need attention, support, faith, and action. In this exercise we're going to start by giving your dream lots of attention.

Exercise 2

As always, sit comfortably with your feet on the floor. Close your eyes and take a few slow deep breaths, becoming aware of your whole body sitting in the chair. Let yourself relax further with each breath. Open your eyes and read on.

State your dream out loud, using the present tense as if it's already happening.

"I am a _____." Or "I am doing _____."

That's pretty good for a first attempt. Now try it again with more enthusiasm. Convince me, and yourself, that this is what you want with all your heart and soul.

How does it feel to say it out loud? Are you experiencing any reactions? If so, write it down. Make note of any gremlins that appeared, and go back to the exercises in the previous section of this book to deal with them if necessary.

Now take some time to imagine your dream in all its beauty. Close your eyes and picture yourself living the dream. Use all your senses to make it real.

- Where are you?
- Who are you with?
- What can you see around you?

- What can you hear?
- Are there aromas or taste sensations?
- How does your body feel?

Take a moment to write down everything you've been experiencing about your dream.

What would make it even better? Imagine the dream expanding beyond your expectations. Write down those thoughts and images, and notice any sensations in your body. Are you feeling happy, excited, or curious? When was the last time you felt like this? Spend some time with this feeling so that it becomes very familiar to you.

Okay, by now you've probably got a few gremlins surfacing, critical voices suggesting that you shouldn't dream so big, that you're just flirting with disaster, and that it's better to keep both feet on solid ground. In order to keep yourself connected to the feeling of your dream, you need an inner champion, an ally who will remind you of that happy excited feeling and drive your gremlins away.

It could be a comic book superhero, a character from a book or a computer game, an animal or bird, or perhaps a cartoon figure. This is the ally that "has your back" and has the power to guard and protect your dream at all cost.

So, who is your inner champion? Write down the idea that comes to mind and feels "right." You can call on your inner champion from this moment on to keep you connected to your dream and moving forward toward the life you want. It will whisper words of encouragement in your ear, give you advice if asked, and uphold your dream no matter what.

Just like the fairy-tale knight in shining armor, your champion will always prevail.

Taking the Leap

It's one thing to have a dream. It's quite another to bring it out of hiding and decide to pursue it. Our dreams seem safer when they're slightly out of reach. We have ongoing conversations with friends about how we always wanted to be or do _____ but couldn't because _____. This seems to put us all in the same boat and gives us something to talk about.

Then, one day, someone in the group decides to take a risk, to actually make a dream come true. The general reaction is often one of dismay and criticism. Why is that? It's because everyone suddenly realizes that they too could have their dreams. But they'd rather stay where it's safe and comfortable, so they try and make that individual conform to the norm once again. However, once you've let your dream loose, it won't fit in the drawer where you've been keeping it for years. It keeps waving its arms, calling to you at night, tantalizing you by day until you simply have to follow wherever it leads.

Deciding to move forward doesn't come without challenges. When we take the slightest step outside our comfort zone, we tend to feel frightened, overwhelmed, and disconcerted. We may want to step back only to find that we can't, so we hover on the edge, between the old familiar world and the new unknown world that is beckoning to us.

Teetering there can feel like standing at the edge of a cliff with a steep chasm below. One tiny slip and we could fall into the abyss, so we cling to the edge of the rock, desperately hoping that a miracle will occur—we'll sprout wings and fly, or we'll wake up and find ourselves safe in bed.

When we're following our dream, it's important to recognize that we will come to edges like this. There are two ways of approaching them. One is to crawl forward and lie immobilized, staring into the vast unknown, stuck between the past and the future. Another is to plan, prepare, and then take a flying leap forward, having faith that you will land on your feet even if you can't see the ground beneath you.

One of my clients provided a good example of this. She was trying to build a new business. While the business was growing, she was supporting herself with income from a job she didn't enjoy. However, it paid the bills so she carried on with it, hoping that one day she would be able to focus primarily on her new line of work. She had been doing this for several years when I began to coach her. She was frustrated and overwhelmed because the time spent at the job was cutting into her ability to develop her business

As we talked, it became clear that she was afraid to let go of the job and the steady income.

"What would you gain by leaving the job and focusing on your business?"

"I'd be able to see more clients."

"And how would that change things?"

"Oh, I'd be a lot happier. And it would probably bring in more money than I make now. But not right away. But what if it doesn't work out? Then what would I do?"

A cloud passed over her face.

I asked her to get up on a chair. She looked puzzled, but climbed up and stood on the chair. I asked her to close her eyes.

"Jump off the chair," I said.

Her eyes flew open.

"I can't do that!"

"Why not?"

"What if I fall?"

"Do you think that will happen?

She looked down at the floor and said, "No. But it feels so scary."

"Well, give it a try and let's see what happens."

She inched closer to the edge of the chair and glanced down again. She closed her eyes and took a deep breath, then opened her eyes again and said, "I can't."

Her fears held her stuck, unable to move forward. It took a few tries and more encouragement, but eventually she managed to jump with her eyes closed. I'm happy to report that she did land on her feet. I suggested she continue to take a "leap of faith" in whatever way she could over the coming week.

"It's a way of reprogramming your brain," I explained. "Taking little leaps becomes easy and normal, so when you're ready to take the leap with your business, you'll be fine."

Edge Surfing

Have you ever watched a surfer ride the crest of a big wave? When it's done well, it's breathtaking—a perfect combination of balance and timing. It also involves courage, determination, and lots of practice.

The changes in our lives come in waves, sometimes little ripples that we barely notice and other times like giant tsunamis that threaten everything we hold dear. It's not the change itself that is difficult for us; it's the transition from where we were to where we're going that's hard.

The line between the old and the new, the familiar and the unknown, is an edge. Everyone deals with edges differently. Some sail over them; others panic and run as fast as they can in the opposite direction.

Exercise 3

For this exercise, you need a notepad and pen.

Ask yourself the following questions and write down the answers:

1. How do you feel when faced with change? Anxious? Excited? Confused? Vulnerable? Empowered?
2. How do you behave?
3. How is this different from your usual behavior?
4. What impact does your behavior have on those around you?

Most people find change stressful and prefer to avoid it at all cost. They might find excuses not to take action, become immersed in other activities, or even become ill. Some people become helpless and let change drag them forward, kicking and screaming. Perhaps you become logical and practical, shut down your emotions, and focus on getting things done.

It's our reaction to change that's stressful. The more we resist, the harder it is on us and on those around us.

Let's make it easier on ourselves!

Draw a line down the center of a piece of paper. On one side of the line, write the word "Now." On the other side of the line, write the word "New" and a couple of words to describe a change you're facing in your life. If you're not currently in the midst of change, then use a situation you faced in the past.

Place the paper on the floor. Stand with your feet on the "Now" side of the line. Think about the way things are now in your life, what you like about it, and what feels comfortable. Make a few notes.

Step onto the line, place your front foot facing forward in the direction of the line, and place your back foot on a slight angle across the line. Imagine you are surfing that edge between the old and the new. Bend your knees; hold out your hands for balance. Think about the things in your life that will be affected when you step into the new situation. Feel the wave of change rising beneath your feet, as your body hovers in the space between the familiar and the unknown. What thoughts and emotions surface? How will you maintain your balance? Make some notes.

Take a deep breath and step over to the new world other side of the line. Imagine how your life will be different. What might you miss about the old ways? What might be better? Write down your thoughts.

When you've finished this exercise, take a few moments to describe your experience in your dream journal. What have you learned about yourself? How do you feel about the change you are facing?

Just Do It

Getting ourselves over the edge, past the change, and into the new situation, is sometimes more than we are willing or ready to handle. It's important to be patient and allow ourselves time to adjust to changing circumstances. However, if we find we're getting stuck, falling back into edge behavior patterns, or crumbling in anxiety, we may need extra encouragement (or a solid push) from people who know us well.

I worked with a woman who had been saying for over a year that she wanted to leave her life in the city and move to a small community in another country. There was a teacher there with whom she had taken summer courses. She dreamed of living there, learning more, and pursuing a new career direction.

Each time she went there for a course, she came back refreshed, energized, and vibrant. After a week back home, however, she would dive into a deep depression. Her friends kept telling her she needed to leave her job and the city because it was sucking the life out of her. She agreed but couldn't find the strength to make the move.

One day, when she was telling me how much she wanted to leave and how good she always felt when she was in this other community, I interrupted her.

"So do it. Don't talk about it, just do it."

"But I can't. My family's here and there's my job, and I can't leave now because we're right in the middle of this project and …"

"Stop," I said. "I've heard this all before. If you want a different outcome, you need to take a different action. So, tell me what you want, in as few words as possible."

"I want to go there, live and work with my teacher, and learn as much as I can."

"When?"

She began to hesitate, so I explained that it's important to commit to a time line for our actions in order to make things happen.

"Okay then, I'd like to be there by November."

We talked about the steps that she'd need to take in order to meet this deadline, and then I asked her to say it again as an intention.

"I intend to leave my job and move there by November," she said in a quiet, trembling voice.

"Stand up. Say it again, only this time loud enough so I can hear you."

She sighed, shrugged, and stood up. She said it again, halfheartedly and a bit louder.

"Hold your arms out, look up, and shout it out, like you really mean it."

She did, with such force that we both burst out laughing.

"Do you really think I can do this?" she asked.

"The important question is, do you?"

We wrote down her action plan, and she committed to taking steps and staying in touch with me about her progress. By November, she had left her job, moved, found an amazing house to rent, and was working with her teacher. Her emails were filled with joy and wonder about the ease of her transition.

Tending the Fire

If you really want your dreams to happen, then you need to be ready to receive the many opportunities that come your way. Your dreamwork for this section of the book gives you a chance to learn more about the art of giving and receiving.

1. Each day find a way to make someone smile. Surprise them with delight: buy a coffee for the driver behind you in the drive-through, toss a coin on the sidewalk for someone to find, compliment a co-worker on their work, thank the cashier at the grocery store, tuck a note into your partner's lunch, give your child an extra hug at bedtime. Note these moments in your journal and the impact the action had on you.
2. Make a note of all the opportunities you have to receive something in the day: a compliment, words of thanks, a cheque, a coupon, a ride, a hug. Notice how you respond. Are you able to say thank you, or do you deflect the offer, downplay it in some way, or give it away?

******

Our dreams, especially the big ones, are like fires that we need to tend with loving care. We feed the fire with small sticks at first, protect it from rain and wind, and gradually build it up so that it blazes with warmth and light. Even tiny embers can grow into a powerful inferno under the right conditions.

When conditions aren't supportive, the fire can quickly go out. One of the fastest ways to douse a fire is to smother it with a heavy wet blanket. There are people in our lives who play this role with our dreams. I'm sure you know a few friends or family members who fit the "wet blanket" description.

These are people who are quick to judge or criticize your dreams and ideas. They roll their eyes at your excitement, shake their heads at your imagination, and caution you to be careful. You may hear comments that echo the words used by your own inner gremlins such as:

"When are you ever going to grow up?"

"You have to be practical."

"This kind of thing never works. Believe me, I know."

They'll tell you that they only have your best interest at heart, they don't want to see you get hurt, or it's better to be safe than sorry.

Why do they do this? Often it's because they're afraid to pursue their own dreams, or they tried once, had a bad experience, and vowed never to try again. If they encourage you to move forward in this "foolish" direction and you succeed, that means they could do the same. And that's too fearful a thought to consider. So they do everything in their power to stop you and keep you trapped in the status quo. Misery loves company!

There are two ways of handling wet blankets in your life. When you're developing a dream, be selective in who you talk to about it. Avoid your critics. In the early stages of dreaming, it's best to spend time with your dream journal and find one supportive person to help keep you on track. This person could be a close friend, a family member, or a coach. Their role is to champion your dream by listening and encouraging you, by providing brainstorming opportunities as needed, and by supporting you to take action toward your goal. Think of this person as a freedom fighter whose sole focus is to set your dream free.

As your dream progresses, you can create a dream network for yourself. This is a group of people who can provide you with the contacts, information, and insights you need to move your dream from dreaming into consensus reality. The makeup of this group is flexible and changes with the needs of your dream.

Time for Reflection

It's time for some quiet reflection. Take your pen and pad of paper and jot down the ideas that come to you as you ask yourself the following questions:

1. Who are the wet blankets in my life? How do they affect me?
2. Who is my freedom fighter? What kind of support do I want from this person?
3. Who do I want to invite to be part of my dream network? Why?

These lists are not cast in stone. Keep adding or deleting names, as more ideas come to you.

Check-in

So, how are you doing? Pause for a moment and check in with your mind and body to see how you're feeling. Are you experiencing any emotions or tension? Are there any gremlins resurfacing? Do you believe in your ability to manifest your dream, or do you have doubts?

Let's take a look at the environment in which your dream is growing. Have you planted the seed yet by writing down your dream? What steps are you taking to nurture and nourish it? Does the dream feel well supported, or is it floundering a bit? Have you been experiencing the suffocating impact of wet blankets, or are you able to spread your wings and fly?

Make a note of how you and your dream are faring at this point. If there are challenges, what steps can you take to resolve them? You might need to set up regular contact with your inner champion, or perhaps you need to give yourself more space from your wet blankets.

Before you go any farther in the book, take steps to deal with the challenges and create the support you need. Otherwise, these issues will continue to trip you up and get in the way of your dream's progress.

Moving into Action

Now it's time to take what you've discovered and put it into action. To develop an action plan, you'll need to refer to the answers you had for the exercises in this section.

In the first exercise, you explored the past to get a better idea of what your secret dream was. There was likely a common thread that wove through your childhood and teenage years, an interest or a passion, a favorite activity that kept surfacing. It may have been a hobby that you enjoyed. When you review the answers to the questions in that exercise, what became clear to you?

1. What have you always wanted to do or be?
This is your secret dream. You might have tried to pursue it at some point in your life, or you may have dismissed it as being impractical or out of reach. For now, just write it down.

Take a look at your answers in Exercise 2. Read your detailed description of your dream.
2. How would it feel to have this dream come true?
Imagine for a moment that you're holding your realized dream in your hands. What emotions are you feeling?
3. What is stopping you from making this dream a reality?
Write down any obstacles or challenges you feel are getting in your way. This may include limiting thoughts, judgmental comments from other people, a perceived lack, and so on. Beside each item on the list, write down one step you can take to overcome it. Remember the tools you've learned in this book already and put them to use (befriending gremlins, working with an inner champion, edge surfing, avoiding wet blankets, creating a support system).
4. Who is your freedom fighter? What kind of support do you need from this person?
Be clear on what you need and then contact this person. Explain the role you'd like them to play and ask them for their support. Establish a regular schedule for updates or meetings by phone,

by e-mail, or in person to ensure that you are fully supported in moving your dream forward.

5. What kind of additional support do you need?

Make a list of areas where you need information, contacts, ideas, or other types of support. Think about people in your circle or your community. Contact them, explain your dream, and ask if they'd be willing to help you by providing a specific item on your list. Commit to regularly updating this dream network and find ways to express your appreciation.

Now let's create your action plan.

In your dream journal, write at the top of a page:

My intention is to (write your dream) *by* (date, month, year).

In order to accomplish this, I commit to taking the following steps:

Make a list of all the steps you can think of that will make your dream a reality. Be sure to include steps to deal with any obstacles or challenges (inner or outer) you are facing. Also list the names of your freedom fighter and dream network and your plan for regular contact with them.

For each item on your list, give yourself a deadline.

Finally, write down the ways in which you'll celebrate your success along the way.

You may wish to set this up in a chart format on the computer so that it's easy for you to refer to. Include a box for checkmarks so you can track your accomplishments. Or go to www.juliewiseconsulting.com/dbx.html and download the exercise package, which includes a chart for this exercise.

Keeping the Momentum Going

Dreams don't magically come true overnight. It takes consistent effort, determination, and confidence to make things happen. By creating an action plan, you have concrete steps to take. Now you need to start taking those steps. Some will be easier than others, but it's important to give yourself credit for everything you do toward your dream. This will help keep you motivated.

In addition, you will need outside support. This is where regular contact with your freedom fighter comes in. This person should have a copy of your action plan in order to check in with you about time lines and give you a boost (or a nudge) if you get off track. Set up a check-in schedule that works for both of you and stick to it. Your commitment to yourself and your dream depends on your ability to keep moving even when you're not in the mood.

Your dream network will also help keep the momentum going by providing you with contacts, information, and ideas. These are people who are well connected in the community, have expertise in the field of your dream, or in areas where you have little knowledge. Don't hesitate to ask for help. That's what they're there for.

The dream is yours. It's up to you to make the commitment to making it a reality. You have to be willing to do what it takes to make it happen.

What are you waiting for?

DREAMMAKERS

Inspiring stories of people
whose dreams make a
difference in the lives of
others

Marie Ens,
Rescuing Those Without Hope

Craig Kielburger,
Free The Children

Marie Ens: Courage and Faith

"Looking back, it might seem courageous, but at the time, it was just the thing to do."

In 2000, following the death of her husband and her retirement from work with the Christian Missionary Alliance, Marie Ens was faced with a choice. She was sixty-six years old. Born in western Canada, she had spent much of her adult life living and working as a missionary in Southeast Asia, primarily in Cambodia. The prospect of spending her retirement years in Canada didn't appeal to her. Yet, going back to Cambodia on her own as a widow was scary. Even though she had survived six evacuations, including a special flight out just before the country fell to the communists, it had always been with her husband, Norm, at her side.

"I look back now and see how, from the beginning, one support after another was taken away," she says. "Family connections because we were in Cambodia, then Norm passing, and finally the Mission. I was being pushed to become more and more dependent on God and His plan for me."

She thought about her options, discussed it with her family, and decided to return to Cambodia.

"I really didn't have any choice," she says. "I knew in my heart that this is what I was meant to do."

Marie began going back and forth between Canada and Cambodia, continuing her work with the AIDS centre opened earlier with another couple. Cambodia has one of the highest rates of AIDS in Asia, including a high percentage of mother-to-child transmissions. Marie remembers when she saw her first AIDS patient. She knew then that this would become her focus.

"The AIDS Centre was the vision," she says. "I never dreamed we'd end up with the complex we now have. I wouldn't have had the desire for a dream as big as this."

In the last six years, the site known as Rescue (shortened from the Cambodian name, which means Rescuing Those Without Hope), has expanded from a few thatch houses for

AIDS families, to a village that incorporates houses for over 200 children who survive their parents, three Baby Houses for children under two, a home for pregnant factory girls, two Granny Houses, a sewing centre, a school for grades one to six, a learning centre with books in Khmer and English, as well as large organic gardens, three fishponds, chickens, and geese. There is another orphanage in northern Cambodia where Rescue has built ten houses for 100 orphans.

The dream keeps evolving as needs arise. Marie marvels at the ease with which resources become available.

"Money has always been there," she says. "As soon as we've thought of something we need to do, the money arrives. It's unreal."

She remembers the time when she and her Cambodian partners decided they wanted to take over ownership of the AIDS Centre. They needed $30,000 to buy out the other founding partners, but they had no money to work with.

"Out of the blue, a friend of mine from the U.S. wrote and asked if we could use some money, without even knowing what we were going through. Her organization wanted to give us $15,000. I burst into tears."

In the early years, the RATANAK Foundation took in funding for Rescue until they were able to set up their nonprofit status. Later, Canadian country and western singer Paul Brandt visited Cambodia with Samaritan's Purse, an international Christian relief agency supportive of Rescue. He became involved in a fund-raiser that raised over $100,000 for the project. It's this kind of unexpected support that continues to amaze Marie.

"I've had the sense of being carried in this," she says. "I don't worry about anything. We never thought that we could do it from the beginning. I'm surprised over and over again at where the support comes from."

She returns to Canada once a year to raise awareness and financial support for Rescue. Her son-in-law, Blaine Sylvester, manages Place of Rescue, a foundation in Calgary, Alberta, that is responsible for fund-raising. However, all of Rescue's staff and committee members are Cambodian.

"The Cambodian people on the committee have the final say in decisions," she explains. "It's important to keep it Cambodian. Let Cambodians manage their own place in their own country. I'm just an advisor."

Blaine comments that he's noticed a change in Marie's perspective in the last year or so.

"When we're on tour, she used to say that she'd retire in ten more years. It was always ten years from whatever age she was then. Last year, she started saying instead, 'I live in Cambodia now.'"

At seventy-six, she continues to be full of vision and energy, constantly involved in the lives of the children, teens, and families who surround her. There is a need to take in more orphans, so she's looking for yet another good housemother to add to the existing staff of about seventy.

When she listens to the youth sing or watches them doing their traditional dances, knowing the horrific circumstances some of them have lived through, she feels overwhelmed by emotion as well as a deep reassurance that this is where she is meant to be.

"God made us with intention, so look into your heart, and you'll see what you're meant to do. What do you love to do? Go in that direction. That's your sweet spot. And that's where I'm living. I feel like I'm the most blessed person in the world."

For more information: www.placeofrescue.com/home

Craig Kielburger: Seizing the Moment

With some dreams, there is a pivotal moment that inspires people to action. Something catches our attention and we know we need to do something about it.

For Craig Kielburger, it happened at breakfast one morning when he was just twelve years old. As he reached for the newspaper, he was looking for the comics. Instead, he found a cause.

On the front page, he saw an article about a young boy in Pakistan. Iqbal Masih had been sold by his parents at the age of four in payment for a debt. He was forced to work at a carpet factory, sitting at a loom and tying thousands of knots every day. When he was ten years old, he managed to escape and began sharing his story throughout Pakistan, raising awareness about the atrocities of child labor. His message gained international attention.

Iqbal was shot to death one day while riding his bike. He was twelve years old.

"When I read that article, I looked at my life, growing up in Canada," Craig says. "Then I thought about Iqbal's life, halfway around the world. Our ages were the same, but everything else was different."

Craig was shocked by the injustice of the situation and tore the article out of the newspaper. He took it to his grade seven class in Thornhill, Ontario, and showed it to them. He told them he had no idea what they could do, but they needed to do something. He asked who would help. Eleven friends volunteered.

That was fifteen years ago. Free The Children has grown to include more than one million youth involved in education and development programs in forty-five countries. The youth involved have built over 500 schools in Africa, Asia, and South America, and provided micro-loans to help more than 23,000 women and their families become economically self-sufficient.

"I don't think any of the twelve who formed Free the Children could have predicted this," Craig says. "Most people tend to think that young people are apathetic to the issues affecting our world. But once we started asking for help, we quickly found thousands of other young people just like us who were eager to change the world."

It was not easy at the beginning though. As a young teen, Craig remembers asking organizations how they could help. Invariably, he'd be asked for his parents' credit card number. Since they couldn't make inroads with existing programs, he and his friends decided to come up with their own projects.

Their premise was threefold: free children from poverty, free children from exploitation, free children from the idea that they are powerless to change the world.

They started by putting together a display for a Youth Week event sponsored by the Youth Action Network. Theirs was the only booth where children, not adults, were speaking on behalf of children's issues. Soon they were touring area elementary schools and high schools talking to other students about child labor. They encouraged children to take action by writing letters challenging companies to make products without using child labor or writing to world leaders asking that more money be spent on education and child protection. As their knowledge about the issues grew, so did their commitment to improving the lives of children around the world. Without realizing it, they were on the path to becoming social activists.

Craig credits his parents with planting the seeds of social justice in his childhood by teaching him and his brother, Marc, about kindness and compassion.

"I remember Mom would take us downtown to go shopping," he says. "We often saw homeless people on the sidewalk. Other people would walk by, but Mom would always stop. As she fished change out of her purse, she'd ask the person's name and how they were doing. The conversation would last no more than a few minutes, but it taught me that everyone deserves kindness."

It's a lesson that sticks with Craig to this day.

Family involvement has always been an essential part of the organization. Marc was a co-founder of Free The Children, and in the early days, the organizational headquarters was the Kielburgers' home and garage. As the brothers grew older, they both chose university programs that would support their work with Free The Children. Craig obtained a degree in Peace and Conflict Studies from the University of Toronto, while Marc graduated in International Relations from Harvard followed by a degree in human rights law from Oxford University.

In addition to being co-founders of Free The Children, Craig and Marc share the director role for Me To We, an organization they founded to encourage ethical living and social responsibility. Me To We includes international volunteer travel programs, leadership workshops, a publishing house, and a line of ethical products. Half of Me To We's annual profits are given to Free The Children, and the remaining half is reinvested.

"Through your daily choices, you can make a difference," Craig explains. "By drinking fair trade coffee or wearing an organic sweatshop-free t-shirt, your actions have an impact on someone somewhere."

He believes that we all have a gift to share with the world. When we combine that gift with an issue that sparks our interest, that's when change happens.

"If your gift is sports, organize a tournament to raise money for cancer research," he suggests. "If your gift is art, donate a painting to a charity auction to end hunger. The possibilities for getting involved are endless."

Craig finds that apathy can be a challenge. However, by bringing youth together and showing them that there are others with similar interests, he hopes to break down barriers and create even more opportunities for change.

In fact, Free The Children offers a wide range of local and international activities for youth, educators, and families to become involved at the level that best suits them. Youth are encouraged to fund-raise, build a school or provide school supplies, or raise community awareness by taking a vow of silence for children who cannot speak for themselves. Teachers can bring in speakers, use related curriculum, or start a classroom group. For families, there's a special kit on making a difference, or the opportunity to volunteer overseas to build a school.

The emphasis remains where it began, however, on youth helping youth.

"There's no better feeling in the world than standing on stage at We Day, surrounded by 16,000 young people who are screaming at the top of their lungs because they are so excited to go out and change the world. If that's not encouragement, I don't know what is."

For more information: www.freethechildren.com
                          www.metowe.com

III

DREAM BIGGER

Rising from the Ashes

"Life is a state of mind." Jack Warden

Picture this. A few months before the Olympics, a world-class skier races down the slope in a practice run in France. She's a medal hopeful for Canada, and suddenly one ski catches on a ripple and she crashes. When the flying snow settles and television cameras zoom in, she's clutching her left knee, clearly in agony.

Her Olympic dream is over—and quite possibly her career as well.

This was the case for Kelly VanderBeek in December 2009. Once the shock wore off, she set her mind to finding ways to make the most of this unexpected change in her plans. She wasn't able to be on the slopes for the Olympic Games, but she was an Olympic Torchbearer (in a wheelchair) and a television commentator for the downhill events. In her blog, she commented that the hardest part of her recovery was letting go of the dream she'd been focused on for so long. Yet, at the same time, she was looking forward to new possibilities that she'd never considered for herself before.

This is a woman who knows how to dream bigger. When the dream you had for yourself has ended, it's time to open up to new dreams.

What would you have done? How would you have handled it?

Okay, so we're not all Olympic athletes. Our tragedies don't necessarily make newspaper headlines, nor do we have the support of an entire nation when we're facing tough times. But life circumstances can knock us flat regardless. Perhaps we didn't dream of an Olympic gold medal, but we all have plans, hopes, and dreams for our lives

Maybe your dream of a marriage that would last forever has come crashing down because of abuse or an affair or the death of your beloved partner. Perhaps you wanted children and the timing or the partner wasn't right, or your body just couldn't make it happen. You might have experienced an accident that changed your life and made it impossible for you to do the work or pursue the passion that meant so much to you before. Did you flee from a war-ravaged county, leaving behind everything and everyone you held dear? Or did your business go bankrupt in spite of your best efforts to keep it afloat?

At some point in our lives, we all face changes over which we have no control. Our "plan" gets swept aside, and we're left with two main choices: try something new or try to reassemble the broken pieces.

Imagine for a moment that you drop a mirror on the floor. What happens? The glass shatters into millions of jagged pieces, scattering in all directions. If you were able to find all the pieces and glue them back together, what would you have? A mirror you couldn't use because the image is fragmented. You're farther ahead to grab the broom and dustpan, sweep up the pieces, toss them in the garbage, and look for another mirror. You can try and find the same style of mirror, or you can look for one that's different, appeals to who you are right now, or suits the decor of your room better than the old one did.

The bigger the crash, the bigger the opportunity. All it takes is the ability to get past the initial shock and look at the options.

So, how do you do that?

It's important to recognize and honor the shock you experience initially. It may take time for you to come to terms with what has changed. Any change requires a grieving period for what has been lost. The time this takes is different for everyone, so be patient with yourself or with someone who's going through this phase.

You'll know you're starting to move forward when your mind kicks in and starts to ask "Why?" The best way to answer this is with another question, "Why not?" These things happen in life. They happen to all of us in one form or another. Why not me? Why not you?

Acceptance arrives when you realize that the change has happened and can't be undone. If this is the new reality, what are you going to do about it? Crying, ranting and raving, feeling depressed are all natural reactions. At some point, however, you'll want to take some sort of action in order to feel like you're in charge again. Even if you can't control circumstances, you can make choices about next steps and that is empowering.

This is where you can apply some of the tools and skills you learned elsewhere in this book. If you look around you, what do you appreciate about your life? Think about the people who've been there for you during this time, the acts of kindness and generosity, the warmth of the sunshine coming through the window, the touch of a loved one's hand, the sound of the birds in the trees, and so on. By noticing the goodness of your life in this moment, you'll open your heart and mind to new possibilities filled with wonder and joy.

Consider what you *can* do, rather than focusing on what is no longer possible. Make a list if that helps, starting with simple activities and expanding it as ideas come to you. Ask close friends for their support and ideas as you create a new path for yourself.

Without realizing it, you're starting to dream bigger. Carry on, accept all ideas as having potential, follow through on suggestions, ask for the resources you need, offer exchanges of goods or services, keep feeding your dream until the details of next steps are clear. Follow them, knowing they will lead you to a life you never imagined for yourself.

Dreaming Bigger

"God gives us dreams a size too big so we can grow into them." Anonymous

In the fall of 2008, I followed one of my big dreams and wandered through Ireland for nearly three months on my own. My grandmother had come from Northern Ireland, and I'd grown up listening to stories of her childhood. I'd promised myself I would go one day, but there were always reasons why it wasn't possible: lack of money, time, family commitments, the thirty years of unrest there, and so on.

However, the one key quality of dreams is that they never really go away. They keep surfacing at odd moments, reminding us of who we are, urging us to move forward and take action.

My life was at a turning point that year. I was alone, divorced for many years, and now my children had left home (and the country) to begin their new lives. There was finally peace in Northern Ireland. However, I was between jobs and although I had the time for a trip, I didn't have the money. The yearning to go became stronger, calling to me during the day, nudging me in my sleep. I kept telling myself it wasn't realistic, or practical.

In late June 2008, I had a vivid dream in which I saw an unusual formation of rocks followed by the words "Giant's Causeway." The next morning, I found the identical image on the Internet along the north coast of Northern Ireland. I knew it was time to go.

In the space of two months, I organized my life so that I could leave for two to three months. I booked my accommodations (including a cottage along the northern coast of Northern Ireland for a month), created a tentative itinerary, sorted out bus and train transportation options, and explored potential hiking and walking opportunities online. I cashed in my retirement savings to cover my costs.

The trip was everything I'd hoped for and more. I met some extraordinary people, had life-altering experiences, connected with the land and my own ancestral roots, and felt truly alive for the first time in many years. Toward the end of the trip, I began to make plans for my future. I decided I would return home, sell my house, and use the money to renovate my summer cottage into a year-round home. I would travel for four months of the year and spend the rest of the year writing about my travels.

What a wonderful dream lay ahead! I was excited about the future because it combined writing and travelling, something I'd been wanting to do for years.

On my last evening in Dublin, I wasn't feeling well. I had been busy that weekend, travelling around, saying good-bye to new friends, and trying to cram in a few tourist sites at the last minute. Around 5:00 P.M., I headed to a nearby restaurant for some soup to see if that would settle my stomach. I didn't make it there.

A passerby found me unconscious on the sidewalk and called an ambulance. I spent two days in a Dublin hospital, undergoing tests. I was told that I'd had two seizures. I was put on epilepsy medication and informed I couldn't drive for at least a year. The doctor told me to make an appointment with a neurologist as soon as I returned to Canada. Additional travelling was not recommended.

My dreams came crashing down around me.

I fumed, ranted and raved at "the Universe" for knocking me off me feet (literally). I'd finally been making a lifelong dream come true, and it wasn't supposed to end this way! I had plans for my future, and I needed to be able to drive to make them work. I also needed to have a clear head if I wanted to pursue my dream of being a writer. The medication was making my mind so fuzzy and sluggish that I could barely manage basic daily functions.

It took me a couple of months to move past my shock and anger. I hit depression when I realized that this situation could be permanent. I didn't know how to pay my bills because I wasn't working. I isolated myself from friends and family. I knew I needed help. However, asking for help meant letting people know I'd been diagnosed with epilepsy, and I was afraid of what they might think.

Finally, in desperation, I sent out an e-mail that changed my life.

I explained the situation briefly to my friends. I said I felt like a butterfly trapped under a heavy blanket, still alive, but barely moving. I asked if they'd be my "butterfly brigade." I imagined them arriving with their beautiful wings fluttering, each taking an edge of the blanket, and together lifting it up and off me so I could stretch my wings and learn to fly again.

The response was immediate and powerful. Friends offered help in myriad ways: giving me rides, phoning or emailing me regularly to break my isolation, suggesting how I could make some money from home, bringing meals, remembering me in their prayers.

People appreciated being asked and were more concerned about me than the diagnosis. It was the beginning of a new phase in my life, one that brought me closer to those around me.

Months passed, I recovered and was able to reduce the medication to a manageable level. I didn't have any further seizures and was permitted to drive again. Between part-time work, a loan from a friend, and other financing, I was able to keep myself afloat financially while I sorted out a new plan for my life. I didn't sell my house and, instead, put my cottage up for sale. I enrolled in a series of training courses in relationship coaching and conflict management, began to develop workshops, write a book, and take on speaking engagements.

When I look back on the seizure episode now, I realize it was actually a gift, an opportunity for redirection. The dream I had for myself wasn't big enough.

It was time to dream bigger.

Reworking the Plan

Life has a way of tripping us up occasionally. Just when we think we have it all figured out, our carefully prepared plan is torn apart and we're left sitting in the scattered remains. If we're particularly stubborn and attached to our "plan," this kind of scenario will likely happen over and over again until we reach the point of surrender.

I don't give up easily, so this was certainly the case for me. In fact, my resistance to change or to an outcome other than what I want made my life path a struggle for many years. I've since realized that it didn't have to be so difficult. Who knew?

If you find yourself sitting in the shreds of the plan for your dream, know that you're not alone. It's a frustrating and upsetting place to be when your situation unexpectedly morphs into something undesirable and unfamiliar. However, remember life moves in cycles and that this too shall pass.

At first, you'll likely need some time to lick your wounds and mope. It's important to grieve what you've lost or what you didn't get to have because the plan changed. It's also important not to spend too much time there. When I work with clients who are in this phase, I usually suggest that they set themselves a time limit for their pity party. It might be twenty-four hours or a week. It's their choice. During that time, they're allowed to fully indulge in their feelings of sorrow, anger, disappointment, frustration, and grief. However, they're not permitted to dump these feelings on anyone else. So they use outlets such as crying, pounding a pillow, going for a run, writing in a journal, talking into a recorder, or dancing it out to loud music. At the end of this set period, they must take a deep breath and face the future, leaving their thoughts of despair behind them.

When things haven't worked out the way we want, one question we often ask ourselves is, "Why?" Why did this have to happen? Why did it happen to me? It's a question that generally has no answer. The time we spend focusing on this question is better spent on considering new directions.

How do we find another direction? The answer may lie in the rubble around your feet. Just like the fabled phoenix, you get a chance to rise from the ashes and create a new way of being in the world. In this section, you'll learn how to expand your vision and take your dream to greater heights than you ever imagined possible.

Unfolding the Messages

We're getting messages all the time from the world around us, but unfortunately we're usually too busy to notice. These are signs, signals, and information that we could use to create a new direction in our lives. All it takes is the willingness to pay attention.

Exercise 1

This is a two-part exercise. You will need a small notebook that you can carry with you during the day.

1. For the next week, jot down things that catch your attention each day. It might be the slogan on bus ad, lyrics from a song on the radio, a bit of conversation you overhear in the cafeteria, a fragrance that awakens a memory, a color in a window display, the way someone walks across the street, the taste of your morning coffee, or the texture of a piece of clothing.

At the end of the week, read through all your entries. Are there any similarities or common threads? Is there a reminder of someone you used to know or something you used to do? Which of the entries excited you most? Circle them.

2. Take a walk, preferably outside. If you can't get outside, then walk through the rooms in your home. As you do, what catches your attention? Stop, notice the details, and then ask yourself these questions:

"What does this item tell me about myself? What does it tell me about my dream?"

Write down the answer in your notebook and continue to walk. When you notice something else, go through the same process. Do this for at least thirty minutes.

Once you have completed this part of the exercise, read the entries. What have you learned about yourself or your dream? If you put the answers for both exercises together, what do you notice?

Try to use this new awareness of your surroundings on a regular basis. You may be surprised at how much you learn about yourself and where you want to go next.

******

Last summer, I did this exercise with a woman who had moved to Canada from another country. We took a leisurely walk outside in the sunshine, wandering through a park, near a lake where seagulls bobbed up and down on the sparkling waves.

I asked her to let me know what leaped out and grabbed her attention as we walked. She noticed the way two trees leaned toward each other and picked up a leaf that had a second one wrapped tightly around it. She commented on the ferry terminal sign and the airplane easing in for a landing at the nearby airport. She also noticed the warmth of the sun on her back and how it felt like she was being hugged.

Each of these signals or signs seemed unrelated to me. To her, however, they brought a consistent message about her family, especially her younger sister with whom she had a close relationship. She realized how much she missed them and that it was time to go home for a visit. Her face lit up at the thought.

"I had been planning to go back sometime next year," she said, "but now I know I need to go back this fall. I'm going to book my ticket this week."

Mining for Gold

How well do you know yourself? Most people have difficulty describing themselves to others. We seem to be taught at a young age to downplay our abilities and expertise. This is why it's often hard to promote ourselves as worthy candidates during job interviews.

If you want to take your dream to the next level, you need to know what you can expect from yourself. You're probably capable of far more than you give yourself credit for.

Exercise 2

In this exercise, you're going to dig deep to discover what you're made of. You'll need a pen and paper.

Set aside some time when you won't be disturbed.

Ask yourself the following questions and write down as many answers as you can. Take your time.

1. What are some of your strongest qualities?
   Imagine that a friend was describing you. What qualities would stand out?
2. What do you value most in relationships, in work, in life?
   Think about what matters most to you, the key components that need to be there in order to make you feel fulfilled.
3. What are you really good at?
   Write down everything you've ever excelled at.
4. What do you love to do?
   If I gave you a billion dollars and you never had to work again, how would you spend your time?

Write a short description as if someone else were introducing you. Start with your name and add in some of the qualities, values, strengths and passions you listed. For example, (*Your name*) is a (*list some qualities*) man/woman who values _____.
He/she is amazing at _____

and loves to spend his/her time _____
_____.

Read that description out loud. Would you like to meet that person? Why? What stands out for you from this description? How many of those qualities, values, strengths, and passions are you currently expressing in your relationships, work, and life in general?

How could you bring more of yourself into all that you do? How would this be useful in moving your dream forward?

Breaking Through

I was recently talking with a woman who had taken a leave of absence from work due to burnout. She had spent the last ten years raising her daughter on her own and working long hours to make ends meet. In the past two years, she'd dealt with the deaths of two close friends and increasing demands at work.

She thought that if she just tried harder, things would get better. But the harder she worked the more her employer demanded, until she was trapped in a never-ending cycle. Her daughter was finishing high school and would soon be leaving to go to university in another city, so she was dealing with that impending loss without having fully dealt with her grief around the deaths of her friends.

"I've always been good at keeping all the balls in the air," she said. "But lately I've been dropping them. I can't seem to get it together anymore."

She explained that she barely recognized herself these days. One minute she felt good and then suddenly she would dissolve into tears. She started to pull away from friends and social engagements, worried that they wouldn't want to be around her because she was so miserable. Each day, it was a struggle to get out of bed. She dreaded going into work to face the growing pile of documents on her desk.

One day her employer insisted that she stay late to finish work on a project. It had been a long week, and she had been counting the hours until she was free to go home. When she heard her employer's words, she burst into tears.

"What's wrong with you?" he asked. "You're behind in your work and you know it's your responsibility to get these files to me on time. Get your act together."

She made an appointment to see her doctor the next day and took a leave of absence.

"I knew I needed some time off," she told me. "I just kept hoping things would get better. Now everyone wants to know how much time I need. I have no idea. All I know is I can't keep going like this."

It has taken time, but with the support of her friends and her coach, she is gradually recovering, rediscovering activities that bring meaning and pleasure to her life. She is also contemplating a career change.

Filling the Well

Do you recognize yourself or someone you know in this story? Burnout is common, especially among people who are highly motivated and committed. Rather than wait to reach the breaking point, it's better to notice the early warning signs and take preventative measures.

Think about times when you're feeling exhausted. There's no pleasure left in life, the focus is on survival, and you become easily irritated and abrupt with those around you. You're not good company, to say the least!

Now remember periods when you've been well rested. There's a bounce in your step and a sparkle in your eyes, you enjoy what you're doing, and life feels great! That's what this book is all about—having more sparkle and less survival in your life.

Exercise 3

Dreams are fed by creativity, and it's hard to be creative when we're exhausted and overwhelmed. It's like trying to get water out of a dry well. If your inner well has run dry, how do you replenish it?

For this exercise, you'll need paper and a pen. Set aside time so that you won't be disturbed.

Sit comfortably with your feet on the floor. Close your eyes and take a few slow deep breaths, becoming aware of your whole body sitting in the chair. Let yourself relax further with each breath. Gently open your eyes and read on.

How do you feel most days? Are you generally relaxed or stressed? Do you sleep well at night or wake up a lot? Jot down your answers.

What are the main stressors in your life? Make a list.

What do you find relaxing and enjoyable? Make a list.

Now take a look at your schedule for the coming week. Which activities listed there absolutely have to happen next week? Which ones can only be done by you?

I'm going to give you two tools to bring joy and balance back into your life and replenish your inner well in the process. They are simple and powerful. One is a word; the other is an art.

1. "No."
2. Delegating

For the next week, practice saying "No" in front of the mirror until you become comfortable with it. When someone asks if you can do something, say "No." One of the ways we exhaust ourselves is by taking on more than we can manage and leaving no time for rest and relaxation. By saying "No" more often, we create time for ourselves.

On your calendar or day timer, cross out any activities that aren't absolutely essential in the coming week. This might mean cancelling invitations, postponing some meetings, or simply deciding not to do something.

Then, practice the art of delegating. Ask someone else to take over as many of the other activities as possible. Perhaps you would do a better job, but let it go.

In all the free time you've now created, write in your name. During those periods of the week, plan to do something relaxing and enjoyable (take a look at the list you made in Exercise 2).

Once you've managed to do this for one week, why stop there? Keep up this habit so that it becomes a normal part of your life. You, and your dream, will be glad you did!

Stepping Off the Merry-Go-Round

Sometimes when we've not recognized the early stages of burnout, we reach a point where the only solution is to take an extended leave from work. If we're lucky, it's our choice. If not, it's because we've succumbed to a serious illness and are forced to take time off to recover. In my case, it was eight long years before I recovered from chronic fatigue syndrome. During that time, I learned a few tips that I'd like to share with you.

While it might seem that stepping off the merry-go-round would be welcome, leaving our carefully structured world behind can lead to new stresses. For the first few days or weeks, you might sleep, read, or rest. After that, you start to feel anxious as if you should be doing something "productive." That is how your world has always functioned, and it's hard to let go of that mind-set, especially if you've been goal-oriented and driven.

This is when you need to remind yourself of the purpose of your time off—to recover from whatever has been causing you to feel overwhelmed and unable to cope. Chances are good that there have been a series of events in your life that have led to your burnout. Some top stressors include birth or death, serious family illness, job loss, financial pressures, and a major change in relationship or residence. Take a look at your recent history and write down the issues that may be contributing to your stress.

What can you do about those matters?

Create an action plan for yourself, just as you have done for your dreams. Come up with specific steps you can take to address the key stress factors. This might include working with a grief counselor or a life/relationship coach, getting financial or career advice, or getting healthcare support.

However, be careful not to fall into your old patterns of trying to accomplish ten of these tasks in one day! Remember that this is your time to rest and take care of yourself, so establish a structure for your day.

Spend part of the day on your action plan, creating it and put it into effect. Then go and enjoy something pleasurable for twice the amount of time you spent being "productive." Try to come up with a few new ideas each week to add to your pleasure list, like having nice dinner by candlelight, dancing in the kitchen to your favorite music, watching an old movie with good friends, or having a pajama party with your kids.

It's easy to slip into depression and isolate yourself from family and friends. Resist this temptation. You do need some time alone to sort things out, but it also helps to be with people who love and support you. Sometimes by reaching out and helping someone else, we start to feel better, so consider how you might help a friend or neighbor once in a while.

Although you may want to curl up on the couch and watch mindless television all day, don't go there! Make a point of getting dressed and going outside every day, for a brisk walk around the block or to the corner store. Exercise helps relax your mind and makes you feel better, so integrate some form of it into your daily schedule.

Even if you're not at work, you can still have a routine and a focus. The difference is that you get to create the structure and choose the goal. Make your goal to become strong, healthy, and happy, and take steps every day to make it a reality.

Making Connections

We are all interconnected, so everything I do affects you in some way and vice versa. Our lives are like ripples in a large pond, spreading out wider and wider, overlapping, interspersing in myriad ways. Once we're conscious of this potential for impact, we can take steps to ensure that it's positive.

Dreamwork

For your dreamwork, you're going to think about the various acts of kindness you give and receive and the impact on the world around you. These acts can be verbal, physical, emotional, psychological, or financial. They can be expected or unexpected, given willingly or with resistance. They include encouraging words and a hug, or the offer of a car ride, a casserole for dinner, or a thoughtful card in the mail.

1. Write down the acts of kindness you've given to others in the past month. What did you do and for whom? How did you feel? Was it easy to do? How did the other person(s) receive it?
2. Now imagine the repercussions each act may have had. For example, if you paid for the coffee of the person behind you in line, he was probably delightfully surprised. Perhaps he had recently moved to your community and has few friends. The gift of a coffee made him feel special and welcome. Imagine that he goes home and tells his wife and children. You've just changed their whole perspective on life in this new community.

As you can see, no action is without consequence. Over the next couple of weeks, notice the acts of kindness and of harshness in your world. Observe what is happening around you at home, at work and in your community. Think of ways you can bring more kindness and joy into the world.

******

We can't do it alone. We all have different strengths and abilities. Hopefully through the exercises you've been doing in this book, you're becoming more aware of your particular strengths and gifts. These are resources that you can use and share, as needed.

Other people have resources that you can tap into as well. All you have to do is ask. Sometimes we hesitate because we see asking as a sign of weakness or an indication that we're not knowledgeable or competent in a specific field. In fact, asking for what we need is a sign of courage, strength, and wisdom. It's an opportunity to learn from someone who has the information we're seeking. It also gives us the chance to offer some of our skills in return. By combining our forces, we are all capable of much more.

For example, I know I'm good at writing. However, I've never taken my writing to the point of being published before. So I set out to find the people and resources I needed to get this book into print. I found a free teleclass that gave me information on setting up the basic structure I needed to stay motivated and keep the writing moving forward. I began to work with a life coach around some issues that were getting in the way of my writing. Through a friend, I found someone who had published a book a few years earlier and was happy to share the details of her experiences with me. I researched several publishing companies, contacted them, and asked further questions. With each step, I learned more and was able to produce what you now hold in your hands. Without these additional resources, this book would still be in draft form, filed on my computer.

I'd like to point out that I didn't start out to write a book. In fact, I was focusing on building my life and relationship coaching practice. The idea for the book came to me one day and wouldn't let go. It was a bigger dream than I'd had for myself, but I followed it, curious to see where it might lead. The book generated speaking engagements, workshops, a series of downloadable one-pagers known as the Wise Living Series, as well as a Web site.

The dream often has bigger plans for us than we anticipate and knows how to connect us to what we need.

Time for Reflection

It's time for some quiet reflection. Take your pen and pad of paper and jot down the ideas that come to you as you ask yourself the following questions. Think about a dream you want to manifest.

1. What strengths do I have that I can use for my dream?
2. What other resources do I need?
3. Where can I find those resources?
4. How can my dream have an even bigger impact?

Check-in

How are you feeling about yourself and your dream now? Excited and inspired? Overwhelmed and discouraged? Take some time to check in with yourself and get an honest assessment of where things stand.

If you're feeling overwhelmed, perhaps it would be good to take a few steps back and consider how you could give yourself some added support. Would it help to chat with your freedom fighter or people in your dream network? Maybe you need some time to focus on other aspects of your life for a while. There is no deadline except the one you choose to set. So take the time you need, move at the pace that works for you, and have faith in your ability to manifest what you want.

It's important to appreciate how far you've come, rather than focusing on how far you have to go. Make a list of all you've accomplished so far and give yourself a big pat on the back. You are a remarkable individual because you've decided to follow your dream. And you're continuing to take steps in that direction, in spite of challenges along the way.

Now take a well-deserved break and celebrate how far you've come!

Moving into Action

It's time to dream bigger! What does that mean? There are a couple of options to consider.

If you had a secret dream and made it a reality by following the steps in the second section of the book, you can now take that dream and make it even bigger. If you didn't do that, or perhaps experienced some setbacks, you can create a new bigger dream now.

For either scenario, the exercises you did earlier in this section will help. Through them, you discovered clues about yourself, your strengths and interests. Review your answers to Exercises 1 and 2 and then consider the following question.

1. What did you learn? How does this information apply to your dream? Is there a new direction beckoning to you?
Write down your thoughts.

When you did Exercise 3, what kinds of ideas began to surface during the free time you created for yourself?
2. How do these ideas apply to your dream?
Jot down your answers.

Now think outside the box. Imagine your dream blossoming and expanding so that it encompasses hundreds or even thousands of people.
3. How can your dream benefit the larger community?
Write down as many ideas as you can. Let your imagination run wild. Don't censor yourself; just keep writing no matter how silly the thoughts might seem to your practical mind.

Now we'll create an action plan. In your dream journal, start a new page and write a brief description of your dream at the top of the page.
"My dream is to _____
_____.*"*

On the next line, write down how you're going to expand upon that dream so that it benefits more people.

"I intend to make that dream even bigger by _____
_____.*"*

Make a list of the potential benefits you've imagined.

What is your motivation for doing this? In order to keep the dream moving forward, you will need strong motivators. List them next.

"I am doing this because _____
_____.*"*

What kind of resources do you need and where will you find them? Make a list of the items required and who your contacts will be.

What steps are you going to take? Be specific and make a detailed list.

How will you reward yourself along the way for all the steps you're taking? Jot down ideas for special treats that you'll enjoy and make a commitment to give them to yourself on a regular basis.

Finally, you need a way to measure your progress. What are the indicators that will show you are moving forward?

"I will know I'm succeeding when _____
_____.*"*

Keeping the Momentum Going

Bigger dreams generally take longer to manifest and require more energy, patience, and perseverance. You need to be determined and focused and try to take at least one step every day toward the dream. The path won't be smooth and easy. You'll be faced with roadblocks, dead ends, and detours. So how are you going to stay on track? You've learned a number of useful tools and techniques throughout this book. To give you a few examples:

- Read through your dream journal and remember why you wanted the dream.
- Create a checklist for your action plan and take pleasure in marking off the steps as you complete them.
- Take time to celebrate all your successes, whether big or little.
- Connect regularly with your dream network and freedom fighter and remember to ask, ask, ask for what you need (a listening ear, resources, ideas or information).
- When things are challenging, take time out and go for a walk, noticing and unfolding the messages that come to you, or find a way to make someone else's day special. It will make you feel good seeing them smile.

It's also helpful to have a physical representation of the dream to keep you focused. It might be a photograph or a drawing that reminds you of your dream. Perhaps it's a quote, or an object like a stone or piece of wood. Just looking at it, or holding it in your hands, reconnects you to your passion and your deep desire to make things happen. Most of all make it fun! Dreaming and manifesting our dreams isn't about struggle and hard work. It's about doing what we love and sharing it with others. So each day find a way to make it easy on yourself, and you'll see that even the biggest challenges are just hidden possibilities waiting to be discovered!

DREAMMAKERS

Inspiring stories of people
whose dreams make a
difference in the lives of
others

David Morley,
Save The Children Canada

Colin and Julie Angus,
Angus Adventures

David Morley: Taking the Leap

Sometimes the dream finds us. We think we're just doing something we enjoy or taking a friend's advice, and we don't recognize that it's the beginning of a path we'll follow for the rest of our lives.

It was mid-1970. David Morley had finished university and was looking for work. He'd enjoyed working at summer camps for low-income developmentally challenged children in previous years, but had no idea what to do next with his life. A friend told him about Pueblito Canada, an international development agency that focuses on improving the lives of children in Latin America. "I'd never thought that much about Latin America," he recalls, "and I thought I was bad at languages, but it meant working with kids who were marginalized from society." He followed the friend's suggestion and headed to Central America to volunteer with street children. His experiences there changed his life. He was shocked by the economic disparities in the region, the extreme poverty, and the circumstances in which the children were living.

"Once I got to know the kids, my dream was that this didn't have to happen to other children," he says. "I asked myself, how can we create a more just economic global system? Or if we can't do that right away, then what can we do to make a difference to a few kids?"

His first challenge was trying to find a productive way to channel his newfound awareness of the issues.

"I remember the first time I came back from Central America. My parents took me out for dinner. I was twenty-two years old and I was angry because Canada seemed so wealthy to me. The restaurant was all shiny and new. The indifference of people to what was happening in other countries drove me to distraction."

He began to look for ways to get the message across. One solution was *Under the Tree: Creative Alternatives to a Consumer Christmas,* a book he co-authored with his wife, Elizabeth. In it, they shared ideas about simpler ways to live, while raising awareness about global environmental and economic issues.

For the next two decades, David continued his work with Pueblito in various countries including Mexico, Nicaragua, and Brazil. Every group he worked with taught him something new. He was in Brazil at the end of the dictatorship, and the focus was on establishing a good daycare system. He remembers the Brazilian women who were struggling to promote the U.N. Convention on the Rights of the Child.

"They taught me about bravery and community organizing, patience and persistence," he says. "And if you can change laws, it can make a difference. But you have to work at the law-making level and the front lines at the same time."

This connection between the frontlines and government ministries was a key lesson that David took with him to the next step in his path. After twenty years at Pueblito, he was finding it harder to be creative, so he felt it was time for a change. He still believed in international collaboration, but wasn't sure what to try next.

One day he happened to see an ad in the newspaper and decided to apply, becoming the executive director of the Canadian section of *Medecins Sans Frontieres*/Doctors Without Borders. He found the new position stimulating and challenging. "I found I could see myself differently," he says. "But it was still the same heart and the same dream."

Over the next seven years, his international experience expanded to include a number of African countries. It was yet another valuable learning opportunity.

"At *Medecins Sans Frontieres*, I learned about the responsibility of being part of a globally recognized organization. You make a tiny noise and it's amplified around the world, so you have to be more subtle about the way you approach things."

Currently, David is the CEO of Save the Children Canada, a position that combines the knowledge gained from his years with *Medecins Sans Frontieres* with his love for children. He feels that one of his main challenges now lies in staying true to his heart while working from a position of power.

"My initial idealism [in his twenties] was to change the world for kids within eighteen months or so," he says with a chuckle.

"As I get older, I find more people listen to me, but I'm also closer to becoming part of the problem. How do I talk to the powers-that-be and still remember the children?"

One of the ways he stays grounded is by talking with trusted friends. Some are volunteers and mentors from Pueblito with whom he has stayed close over the years. Another is a group of friends he's played hockey with once a week for thirty years. He stresses that if you don't have a good support system, the enormity of the task will seem overwhelming. With support, however, you don't even notice the size of the task at hand.

He also finds inspiration in the people he works with.

"When I was in the Republic of Congo," he says, "some of my colleagues were shrugging and saying, 'Yeah, so we've had a civil war. But we're going to make our country better!' I find the people and partners so inspiring that I have no choice but to continue to find ways to support them."

With each step along his path, he has appreciated the opportunities to meet people and learn more. Even though he didn't recognize it at first, he now sees that he was following his heart from the start. For him, this is one of the key points to keep in mind when choosing your path.

"I know when I'm following my heart because I'm happier," he explains. "I can feel something singing inside me."

However, he's quick to caution against being naïve.

"Do your analysis. Be realistic, but still do it. Do it with an open heart."

David has come to accept that changing the world is not going to happen as quickly as he, or others, might want. He now sees the process as a marathon relay race in which we all need to work together for the sake of the bigger vision.

"Share the dream," he suggests. "Put all ego aside and pass the baton. If everyone does their part …"

For more information: www.savethechildren.ca
                         www.msf.ca
                         www.pueblito.org/index.html

Colin and Julie Angus: Sharing the Journey

Dreams take us on a journey into unknown territory, challenging us to try new things, pushing us beyond perceived limitations. We gain awareness of ourselves and our abilities as unexpected setbacks and detours force us to dig deep and find creative solutions. Sometimes, if we're lucky, we find someone who shares our exhilaration and keeps us motivated when times are tough.

Colin and Julie Angus know all about pushing themselves and their relationship to the limit. The young Canadian couple is making a career of exploring the world using human-powered forms of transportation: cycling, rafting, rowing, sailing, and hiking. Even though they were both fascinated by adventure books as children, they never imagined that one day they would be writing books about their own expeditions, inspiring a new generation of readers and dreamers.

At the age of twelve, Colin read a book about a sixteen-year-old boy who had sailed around the world on his own. He decided he'd like to do that one day, so he began saving money from his paper routes. After graduating from high school, he bought an old sailboat with a friend, fixed it up, and with sailing experience gleaned mostly from books, headed out across the Pacific. He spent five years sailing the Pacific Ocean, three of them on his own, before deciding he was ready for a new challenge.

In 1999, with two colleagues, he set out to cross South America from the Pacific Ocean to the Atlantic. This involved hiking 200 kilometers from the Pacific coast to the source of the Amazon River and then rafting and paddling 7,200 kilometers down the length of the Amazon to the Atlantic Ocean. The five-month journey unexpectedly opened doors to a new way of living.

"I didn't think it could be a career," he says. "I just had the desire to see the world. But after the Amazon trip, I wrote a book and made a film. We sold the film to the National

Geographic Channel. It didn't make a lot of money but it was enough to motivate me to go out and do it again."

Meanwhile, Julie was busy pursuing a career as a molecular biologist. Although she enjoyed outdoor activities, she didn't see herself as a career adventurer. The two first met at a bus stop, when Colin was in the midst of preparations for what he hoped would be the first human-powered circumnavigation of the world. With a colleague, he planned to trek, cycle, ski, and canoe across seventeen countries, as well as row across both the Atlantic and Pacific Oceans.

"It probably wasn't the best ingredient to throw into a fledgling relationship," he says with a chuckle. "But it did give us a chance to learn a lot about each other."

As it turned out, Julie was looking for a challenge. She'd been thinking about rowing across the Atlantic with a girlfriend, but had discounted it at first because she didn't feel she had the skill set. Watching Colin prepare for his journey and seeing all the steps he took to ready himself inspired her.

"I realized I could learn about open ocean crossings," she says, "and I could learn to row."

She began to prepare and plan, starting to train with her friend when Colin left on his two-year expedition. When her girlfriend changed her mind, Julie continued to train on her own. By this point, Colin's colleague had pulled out of his expedition, and Colin was trekking solo across Siberia.

"He was looking for an expedition partner," Julie recalls, "so it made sense to combine our journeys."

She completed the second half of the expedition with him, including the five-month row across the Atlantic, becoming the first woman to row the complete Atlantic from mainland to mainland.

Even though they had meticulously planned the ocean crossing for a time when hurricane risk was low, the weather had other plans. They were about three weeks out in the ocean when a storm began to brew. The water grew deadly calm and then the wind and waves began to rise from all directions. Julie and Colin secured everything, nailed the hatches closed, and sequestered themselves in the tiny cabin. They thought it was just an ocean storm until Julie called her father on the satellite phone and heard that a hurricane was tracking toward them. It was a part of the Atlantic where there had never been a hurricane before.

"We were in the cabin for three and a half days," Julie says. "We rode out fifty-foot waves and winds over 120 kilometers per hour. We were bruised, dehydrated, and exhausted."

Looking back, she credits their success to being able to work as a team.

"It makes a big difference having someone there to hear your fears," she says. "The anticipation was tough, but we talked about different scenarios so we could be as prepared as possible."

Colin echoes her thoughts, thinking back to the time he was separated from his colleagues in a remote part of Mongolia for twelve days. They were partway through their attempt to become the first people to run the Yenisey River from source to sea.

"It's important to be prepared and to take steps ahead of time," he says. "You can envision most things that might happen. And once something occurs that you weren't anticipating, you take stock of what you have, get inventive, and recruit the help of others."

While they clearly rely on each other for much of the support they need during expeditions, they stress the importance of having friends and followers to provide encouragement.

"It means a lot to know that people believe in you," Julie says. "Just hearing that friendly voice on the phone can make a difference."

People who follow their adventures through their Web site, e-newsletter, or growing number of books often offer information they find useful in planning the next expedition.

"People who've been there share their experiences with us," Colin says. "We navigate our way through new waters based on their advice."

As with any dream, there are good days and bad days. Colin suggests it helps to try and maintain a positive outlook by reminding yourself that there will be better times ahead.

"When you're stuck in the mud in the pouring rain in the middle of nowhere and you're running out of food, it takes a lot of effort to keep motivated," he says. "You just want to crawl into your sleeping bag and not get up. But you have to try and isolate yourself from your feelings and put one foot in front of the other and keep going."

Julie points out that the preparation can take just as long, if not longer, than the journey itself. She feels it's time well spent because it helps you gain confidence in your abilities and strengthen your skill set.

Although advice from others may be valuable, they stress the importance of doing your own homework to make sure that the information you're using is accurate. It's also key to listen to your heart and not be dissuaded by naysayers.

"There are people who'll tell you that you won't succeed," Julie says. "Recognize that. What you learn from taking the journey is important, whether or not you achieve the dream."

The two are already busy finalizing details for their next expeditions. In June 2010, Colin planned to row around Vancouver Island in sixteen days or less in order to beat the seventeen-day record held by a British kayaker. To follow up on their 2008 rowing and cycling journey from northern Scotland to central Syria, Julie is currently organizing a return to Syria in 2011. They'll trek across the desert and explore the olive-growing region where her family comes from.

"There are always lots of ideas," Colin says. "The fun is thinking about all the different possibilities."

For more information: www.angusadventures.com/index.htm

CONCLUSION

Dreamer, Know Thyself

"Why not be oneself? If one is a greyhound, why try to look like a Pekingese?"
Dame Edith Sitwell

Once upon a time, in a barnyard far away, a nest of eggs hatched. One of the ducklings was different from the rest and the contrast became more apparent as the ducklings grew bigger. The other ducks thought he was ugly and teased him mercilessly. The ugly duckling did his best to swim and quack like the rest of the ducks, but to no avail. His voice was louder and deeper, his feet were bigger, and his neck just kept growing longer until he towered over the others.

He was eventually chased away from the farm and wandered the world, lost and alone. No matter where he went, he didn't fit in. Somehow he survived the winter, and in the spring when the ice melted on the rivers, he heard a beautiful sound in the air. He glanced up and saw a flock of graceful white birds coming in for a landing nearby. They had long necks and deep voices. Mesmerized, he swam closer wanting to get a better look. To his surprise, they didn't chase him away, but welcomed him in. When he glanced down into the river, he was startled to see that he had become like them—a swan.

How much of your life has been spent trying to fit in? Did you feel like you didn't belong in your family of origin? Did you have to conform to certain behaviors or attitudes in order to get their approval? What about once you started to work? Did you find work that truly suited your skills and personality, or did you get a job to pay the bills?

Society isn't kind to people who are different from the norm. We're quick to judge others, labeling them as eccentric, a black sheep, or unconventional. We also tend to shun such individuals as if we're afraid their unacceptable behavior will be contagious.

Creative people are often more expressive and vibrant than others. They also tend to bend rules, attempt the impossible, and take risks, just to see what will happen. The same is true for people who follow their dreams. In order to make your dreams come true, you have to break the rules that say you shouldn't, ignore the voices that say you can't, and push past all the obstacles that stand in your way. It takes a lot of courage to do this, especially if you're surrounded by people who believe dreams can't come true.

Are you ready to take the plunge and pursue your dream, knowing that you might get more criticism than encouragement from family and friends at first? How important is your dream to you? Are you willing to make it a priority and do whatever it takes to make it happen?

The ugly duckling didn't dream of becoming a swan, but his instincts told him that he didn't belong where he was. So he followed his heart, and it eventually led him home, to a place and a group where he was honored and respected for who he was. It wasn't a quick or easy journey, there were challenges along the way, but he kept his webbed feet moving steadily toward the future.

Are you a swan living in a duck's world? If so, you may have disguised yourself well by learning duck talk and perfecting duck walk. However, you're only fooling yourself, because everyone else can see quite clearly that you're really not a duck. When are you going to give yourself permission to be who you truly are?

If I were to hold up a mirror in front of you, what would you see? Are you happy and content with your work and relationships? Is your life heading in the direction you want? Are you on track with your goals and aspirations?

Whether you answer yes or no, what if life could be even more? More joy, more ease, more freedom. What if *you* could be more?

I believe we all come to this earth with unique gifts. Our task is to discover these gifts, develop them fully, and share them with the rest of the world. First, however, we have to get to know ourselves. Our strengths, values, and passions hold the key to our gifts. That key unlocks the door to our dreams.

Once we walk through that door, a new world of unexpected opportunities awaits.

The ugly duckling had to acknowledge to himself that he was a swan before he could find a supportive circle. What is it about your nature that makes you a swan? Are these qualities that you value and respect in yourself and in others? How can you bring more of those qualities into your everyday life, at home, in your relationships, and at work? You don't need to emerge from the shadows overnight. In fact, you can take as much time as you need to shed your disguise and step forward in all your glory. Just keep taking steps, and you'll get there.

As you do, you'll find that like-minded people are drawn to you. Your network will begin to change, and you'll find out about people, places, and activities that are a good fit with what you love to do. It may surprise you how quickly this happens. It all starts with a conscious choice on your part to honor the dream inside you that wishes to be heard.

It takes time to transform yourself and your life. It didn't happen overnight for the ugly duckling. He had to go through the natural growth process as soft baby down was gradually replaced by grey feathers and then the brilliant white of the adult swan. Each step along your path is an important part of your growth process as well.

Celebrate your successes, keep your eyes focused on the dream, move those feet steadily forward, and watch for other swans along the way!

AFTERWORD

It's All About Trust

"When I'm trusting and being myself ... everything in my life reflects this by falling into place easily, often miraculously." Shakti Gawain

I have to admit that I put off writing this section of the book for a couple of weeks. In fact, when I sat down this morning to write, my mind was blank. And then it hit me. In order to write about trust, I needed to trust—that the ideas and words would come.

When we're pursuing a dream, it's important to recognize that it's a process; a journey not a destination. We need to trust that process, especially when we don't know what to do next. We may even question if we're heading in the "right" direction. Those are the moments when doubt kicks in, and it's up to us to make sure that trust is not far behind.

But what do we trust in when all the usual guideposts are gone? Where do we find the courage to keep taking steps in the dark?

This is when it's important to know yourself well because inside your heart there is a still, quiet place that holds all the wisdom you will ever need. It's a connection to what I call your inner Dreamweaver, a place that holds your dream as sacred. When you make decisions from that space, the outcome will always be for the Highest Good of all concerned, even if it's not clear in the moment.

The feeling in that place is different for everyone. For me, it's a deep sense of knowing. I can't explain it because there are no words. I simply *know*. I've heard others talk about how their heart sings or how suddenly their vision clears and they can see only one obvious choice.

There isn't any secret door or magical chant for getting to this place of wisdom. With my clients, I usually suggest a form of meditation. By focusing on their breathing, they slow down their mind's chatter and then take their awareness into their heart area. Once there, I'll ask a simple question about what they need to know. They say out loud the first thought that surfaces. The Dreamweaver's answers are always to the point and sometimes even amusing. The heart knows; it's our mind that gets in the way.

At times, I've found a walking meditation helpful. I'll head out for a brisk walk by myself, often in a wooded area so I can be alone with nature. With each step, I try to empty my mind of thoughts and gradually open up to what's happening around me. If I see a butterfly, I'll stop and pay attention to its beauty. I'll pause to notice the view over the river from the top of a hill. The songs of the birds and rustling of chipmunks in the leaves will also capture my awareness. Once I realize that my mind and body are calm, I find a spot to sit and go deep into my heart to ask for guidance. The answer doesn't always come right away, but once the question is planted, I know the response will surface, usually before I arrive back home.

Another approach is to create a mental image of your inner Dreamweaver and get to know him or her well. What kind of clothing does she wear? What are his favorite foods? Does she like to dance or sing, or perhaps camp and canoe? Once you've developed a strong sense of who this being is, then it's time to build your relationship. Remember that the sole purpose of your inner Dreamweaver is to support you in making your dream a reality, so the more you work together, the easier it will become to manifest your dream.

With this in mind, try to spend time with your Dreamweaver every day. Sit down in the morning, close your eyes and slow down your breathing, and imagine your Dreamweaver is sitting in the room with you. Ask for guidance about next steps, and listen for the response. Sometimes it helps to get up and move over to where the Dreamweaver is sitting in order to voice the response more easily.

The answer may not be what you're expecting. I'll give you an example.

One day I asked my Dreamweaver what steps to take that day toward moving my coaching business forward. I was anticipating a practical to-do list. Instead what I heard was:

"Take a nap."

"What?"

"I said, 'Take a nap.'"

"But, but, but …"

I could think of countless reasons not to lie down, all very practical and urgent. However, I was very tired because I had been pushing myself a lot lately to make things happen. So I had a nap. And as I woke up, my mind cleared, and I suddenly had a series of brilliant ideas for expanding my business.

Even if the answer isn't what you want or think will work, follow the guidance. It shows you're starting to trust your Dreamweaver as a valued partner. The more you trust, the more guidance you'll get, and each time the answers will come more easily and clearly.

The trust muscle is like any other in your body. It needs to be exercised regularly. One way of doing this is to practice trusting on the small issues before you get to the big ones. Start by expecting good things to happen. Trust that you'll find a good parking space, and if you don't, trust that there's a good reason you didn't. Perhaps someone else needed that space more.

As you can see, trust is closely linked to acceptance, another challenging concept for many people. Acceptance doesn't mean resignation. It means seeing the situation as it is in this moment and determining how to move forward from there. Things don't always work out the way we want them to. Rather than sink into frustration and anger, we can choose to accept and then trust that there's something better up ahead.

A few years after my marriage ended, I had to sell my house for financial reasons. It was a dream house, one built with loving attention to detail, sunlight streaming through the rooms, warm pine woodwork and tile floors, and breathtaking gardens. There was even a secret garden with roses and a meditation area. It was also the house my children had grown up in. The decision to sell was, therefore, a very difficult process for me.

I knew I had to move, but my heart wasn't in it. Together with a realtor I searched for a new place for months. I couldn't find anything that felt right. After about three months, I became very discouraged. I decided to go out and buy something for my new home even though I didn't know where it was yet. I needed something to keep me inspired. I found a gorgeous comforter for my future bedroom. I loved the warm earth tones and subtle patterns. Just looking at it made me happy, and that shifted my perspective on the moving process. With that comforter in my bedroom, the next house was bound to be wonderful.

Shortly after that, I bought a semi-detached house that needed some work. Over time, I transformed it into an urban oasis, and it turned out to be the perfect home for me, and my children, for the next seven years.

The timing for our dreams isn't always what we'd like it to be. We can do all the planning and take all the steps we want, but in the end, we have to allow things to unfold in their own time. That's not easy to do. When we finally know what we want and we've figured out how to make it happen, we want the result now. Today. Sooner if possible.

But if we try to rush the process, we could make things far more difficult for ourselves than necessary.

I currently live in a condo townhouse. Over the past few years, the management company has been replacing the front doors. I knew that mine was due to be replaced this spring at no cost. Since I plan on moving, I saw this as an unexpected bonus—a fresh new door to greet potential buyers.

For several months, I've been gradually going through cupboards, boxing up items I no longer use, and giving them away. I have a to-do list for repairs and repainting in preparation for putting the house up for sale. Last week, for example, I paid to have the front door locks rekeyed so that the same key would work in both the upper and lower doors. It was almost the last item on my list, and I was very pleased with myself for being so well organized.

Yesterday, my new upper door was installed. As the contractor was leaving, he handed me a key. "Your old lock doesn't fit this door," he said, "so I had to put a new one in. Here's the key."

It brings to mind the saying: if you want to make God laugh, make a plan.

This is not to suggest that we shouldn't make plans or take action. In fact, moving our dreams forward depends on that. However, we also need to be open to trusting that there are more factors involved than we realize. Some doors need to close so we can be rerouted and the timing may be different than we envision.

Trust gives us the strength to let go of the familiar and take the leap into the unknown as we begin the journey toward our dream. It also holds our hand and murmurs reassuring words along the way when we lose faith, get discouraged, and mutter to friends about how what we left behind is starting to look better every day. As doubt and fear creep into our minds, trust is there, jumping up and down trying to get our attention, reminding us that the best is yet to come, if only we believe.

"Just a little bit farther," it shouts, while doubt and fear cast shadows across our vision, plotting the demise of our dream.

What do you do when you can't see your way clearly any longer? Perhaps a few too many doors have closed and you've lost your way. Or well-meaning friends and family have suggested one time too often that you're tilting at windmills and it's time to be "realistic."

It's time to go back to the beginning and the reason why you started on this path. What was your vision and why was it so important to you? Has that vision shifted in some way, or have you simply lost touch with the essence of it?

If you're feeling stuck, take a break and do something else for a while. Tunnel vision is not conducive to dream building. Your dream is supposed to be something you enjoy and are passionate about, so if pursuing it has become a chore, that's a signal that something's off. Spend time with inspiring people, do something you've never done before, shake up the routine, and then come back to your dream.

I've noticed that the Universe is always offering me little signs of encouragement. If I'm paying attention, I see them and gain a fresh perspective on my situation. It might be a song I hear in the grocery store or a slogan on a t-shirt. When something catches my eye, I ask myself how it might apply to my dream.

For example, the other day I took a walk along a nearby creek because I needed a break from writing. It was a beautiful spring day, with a bright, blue sky overhead, gentle breezes rustling through the trees and birds happily singing along the path. As I walked, I was mulling over a chapter in this book that I was stuck on. I really wanted to get it finished but I couldn't figure out what to do next.

I glanced at the creek where it bends around a corner and disappears from view. Standing motionless in the water behind a partially submerged tree trunk was a great blue heron. It seemed to notice me at the same moment. We stood and stared at each other. Then, slowly and methodically, the heron began to move forward, lifting one long leg at a time with great effort, carefully finding its footing before taking the next step. It paused and turned its body toward me, extending its neck to watch me from above the tree trunk. After a while, it resumed its original stance, waiting patiently and motionless as only a heron can.

As I walked on, I realized that the heron had provided the answer I needed. I'd been trying to rush the writing process. But the message from the heron was:

Be patient. Let the fish (or ideas) come to you.

Are things taking longer than you had hoped? Instead of fuming about how far you still have to go, appreciate what has been accomplished so far. Take a look at all the support you've received, the steps you've taken, and the courage you've shown. Perhaps you can take a look at your action plan and pick one more item to tackle today. Give yourself a big pat on the back for a job well done.

It helps to keep in mind that the darkest moments tend to come just before the dawn. I have a good friend who patiently reminds me of this whenever I'm lamenting the lack of progress I'm making with my dreams. I seem to have to go through a breakdown right before a breakthrough. She has watched this happen so many times that she knows my deep discouragement is a sign I'm about to break free and move forward with lightning speed. Just knowing this shifts my perspective and helps me see that the downward spiral is actually part of my forward process.

Find a way to recommit to your dream, especially if your motivation is sagging. Remember the comforter that I bought for the bedroom in a house I hadn't found yet? In any journey, it's essential to have touchstones to help us keep the faith along the way. What can you do to show you believe your dream is going to happen? Believing in the dream and committing to the process by taking action has far more power than you may realize. It brings into play forces beyond your knowing, and this leads to magic and miracles. Think of this step as giving yourself a personal talisman or a dream token for your journey.

When all else fails, one action that always reinspires me is to do something to support someone else with their dream. It takes my focus off myself and my challenges, and reconnects me to my heart. From there, it's a quick and easy journey back to the beginning, to the joy and passion that ignited my dream in the first place.

And then I'm off and running once again.

About the Author

Julie Wise is a life and relationship coach who works with people around the world to realize and achieve their dreams. As a motivational speaker and freelance writer, she brings a positive message to audiences, drawing on her innate wisdom and personal life experiences. Her training is in organizational and relationship systems coaching, as well as in conflict management and mediation. A former newspaper columnist and editor, she has now published the Wise Living Series, offering simple tips for bringing more joy and ease into all aspects of life. It is available as a free download on her Web site at www. juliewiseconsulting.com. She also keeps a blog with regular updates, which you can follow through her Web site.

Julie lives in Waterloo, Ontario, Canada where she is currently dreaming even bigger.

Dream BIGGER
Exercise Package

Eager to do the exercises?

Here's a way to keep all your creative ideas together in one place!

Created just for you, easy-to-use PDF files of the exercises in each section of the book, giving you ample room to let your thoughts flow. Also included, one BONUS exercise not offered in the book.

Free download at:

www.juliewiseconsulting.com/dbx.html

Wise Living at your fingertips!

A series of downloadable easy-to-follow guidelines for making simple changes to create the life, work and relationships you've always dreamed of! The series is divided into three categories: relationships, life transitions, work/career issues. And the best part is that they're **FREE!**

Relationships
Are you ready for great relationships at home and at work? These helpful tips will stimulate your creativity and breathe new life into your personal and work connections.

Life Transitions
Have you been challenged by one of life's curve balls? Check out these ideas for navigating change with courage and conviction.

Work/Career Issues
Are you facing a rocky road, detours, or a dead end at work? This series offers some secrets for success on the career path.

Available as free download at:

www.juliewiseconsulting.com/products.html